CHRIST
PRECIOUS

To Those That Believe

JOHN FAWCETT

POSITIVE ACTION FOR CHRIST
CLASSIC REPRINTS

Written by John Fawcett
Layout and Design by Shannon Brown

Positive Action For Christ, Inc., P.O. Box 700, 502 W. Pippen, Whitakers, NC 27891. Printed 2005.

ISBN: 1-59557-023-3

Published by Positive Action For Christ, Inc.

Foreword

The burden of Positive Action For Christ is to help Bible teachers magnify the majesty of God. To that end, this classic reprint has been published. Nowhere have we found a book that so magnifies the beauty of Christ as this magnificent treatise on "faith and love."

John Fawcett states in his introductory remarks, "Without a sincere attachment to the Author of eternal salvation…whatever works of morality we may perform, our obedience will be materially and essentially defective, as not flowing from a proper principle."

He could not have stated it better. Obedience flows from a genuine love for the precious Savior. As Wilberforce puts it, "The fatal habit of considering Christian morals as distinct from Christian doctrines, has insensibly gained strength….and…the moral system itself also began to wither and decay." If that was true in the early 1800's, what must be true today?

Much of today's preaching is moralistic and behavioristic at best. Pastors and youth leaders urge their flocks to obedience, when in reality they are being conformed to a lifestyle. Though the lifestyle is commendable, it is too often driven by outward pressure and inward guilt rather than the constraint of love for God. Such outward conformity is actually behavior and not obedience. As Fawcett so richly declares, obedience must flow from a "proper principle" and that proper principle is boiled down to its essence in Christ's question, "Lovest thou me?"

Fawcett says that by contemplation of Him, faith lives, all the springs of repentance are opened, love is kindled into a holy flame, sin is mortified, the world is subdued, and "the hope of future glory is confirmed." What else do we need? It is our prayer that this classic will impact your heart and the hearts of those to whom you minister in this way.

Contents

Chapter One

Introductory Remarks

The subject to which the reader's attention is invited in these pages is of the highest importance; since love to the divine Redeemer is the distinguishing characteristic of a real Christian, and most indispensably requisite, in order to our serving God acceptably in this world, and to our dwelling with Him in the next. Without a sincere attachment to the Author of eternal salvation, whatever works of morality we may perform, our obedience will be materially and essentially defective, as not flowing from a proper principle.

Love is the parent and promoter of every thing excellent and amiable in the Christian character. It diffuseth itself through the whole train of holy actions. It gives them all their motion, and dignifies them with all their real value. The eloquence of men, or even of angels, the gift of prophecy, the knowledge of all mysteries, the power to work miracles, the most extensive liberality to the poor, and even the suffering of martyrdom, are all insignificant and unprofitable without love.

He who loved us so as to give Himself a ransom for our souls, who was lifted up upon the ignominious cross, that He might draw all men unto Himself, proposes to those who profess to be His disciples, the solemn and important inquiry, "Lovest thou Me?" He values not our service if the heart be not in it. He knows what is in man; He sees and judges the heart, and has no regard to outward acts of obedience, if no devout affection be employed in them. It is not enough for the eye to be lifted up to Him, or the knee to bow before Him; it is not enough for the tongue to be employed in speaking of Him, or the hand in acting for His interest in the world. All this may be done by those whose religion is mere pretence. But the heart with all the inward powers and passions of the soul, must, in the first place, be given to Him. "Grace be with all them that *love* our Lord Jesus Christ in *sincerity*;" and as the natural consequence of that, keep His commandments.

I would ground the following observations on the words of the apostle Peter:

---

1 PETER 2:7

Unto you therefore which believe He is Precious.

The word *precious*, is a substantive and signifies honour, price, or preciousness itself; that which is of infinite value.

The persons to whom Christ is precious are, with great propriety, said to be those that believe. Unbelievers see no form or comeliness in Him, nor any beauty that they should desire in Him. Hence have we so many strange notions advanced concerning His adorable Person. Many daringly deny the only Lord that bought us with His own dear life, and substitute a mere creature in His room. There are others who have such low and irreverent conceptions of Him, as if they knew not the use of His person, His work, and His sacrifice, in the business of our salvation. Whereas there is nothing in our religion which hath either truth, reality or substance, but by virtue of its relation to Christ and what He has accomplished on earth on our behalf.

Perhaps in no age, since the establishment of Christianity in the world, was greater opposition made to the real dignity and glory of the Son of God than in the present. It is a consideration which may justly affect the hearts of all that love Him in sincerity. The doctrine of His proper Deity is the ground of all our hope and salvation by Him, and the very foundation of the Christian religion; yet the disbelief of this is openly avowed by many, who strenuously maintain and industriously diffuse their sentiments in the world.

It is awful to consider, how many ruin their own souls by stumbling on the rock of safety, and dash themselves in pieces on that which is laid as the only foundation of hope. Yet in this the Scripture is fulfilled. The same Jesus, who is precious to them that believe, is "a stone of stumbling, and a rock of offence, even to them which stumble at the word, being *disobedient.*" The reason here assigned why men stumble at the word, and at what it reveals concerning Jesus Christ, is disobedience; and, perhaps it will be found, that, in many instances, the cause of men's rejecting the Saviour, is, a rooted aversion to that purity of heart and conduct which the evangelical system requires. "This," says our blessed Lord, "is the condemnation, that light is come into the world, and men love darkness rather than light, because their deeds are evil."

Christ is not precious to those who do not, under a sense of their absolute need of Him, manifest that regard for Him which the sacred Scriptures every where require. The religious system, adopted by many at this day, has very little of real Christianity in it. Many laboured performances are now published to the world, in which we find the duties of morality recommended with peculiar elegance of style, and acuteness of reasoning, wherein we meet with little or nothing concerning the person, the work, or the grace of our Lord Jesus Christ. This is like raising a superstructure, without a solid foundation. The great mystery of redemption by the blood of that Lamb of God which taketh away the sin of the world, appears to be of little or no use with such persons, in their attempts to promote piety and obedience.[1] There may be many things in such performances highly worthy of attention; there may be a striking display of learning and ability; but at the same time, that which constitutes the real essence of Christianity, and which is the proper spring of all true obedience, is entirely omitted.

"It is not so," says a very respectable writer of the present age, "it is not so in our view of things. We find so much use for Christ, that He appears as the *soul* that animates the whole body of our divinity; as the centre of the system, diffusing light and life to every part of it. Take away Christ, and the whole ceremonial of the Old Testament appears to us little more than a dead mass of uninteresting matter; prophecy loses almost all that is interesting and endearing; the gospel is annihilated, or ceases to be that good news to lost sinners, which it professes to be; practical religion is divested of its most powerful motives; the evangelical dispensation of its peculiar glory, and heaven itself of its most transporting joys.

"The sacred penmen appear to have written all along upon the same principles. They considered Christ as the all in all of their religion, and as such, they loved Him with their whole

---

1 A modern writer, of distinguished eminence, justly remarks, that towards the close of the last century, divines professed to make it their chief object, to inculcate the moral and practical precepts of Christianity; but without sufficiently maintaining, often even without justly laying the grand foundation of a sinner's acceptance with God; or pointing out how the practical precepts of Christianity grow out of her peculiar doctrines, and are inseparably connected with them. By this fatal error, the very genius and essential nature of Christianity underwent a change. She no longer retained her peculiar character, or produced that appropriate frame of spirit by which her followers had been characterised.—*Facilis descensus.*

The example thus set was followed during the present century, and its effect was aided by various causes. The fatal habit of considering Christian morals as distinct from Christian doctrines, has insensibly gained strength. Thus the peculiar doctrines of Christianity went more out of sight; and, as might naturally have been expected, the moral system itself also began to wither and decay, being robbed of that which should have supplied it with life and nutriment. At length, in our own days, these peculiar doctrines have almost altogether vanished from the view. Even in many sermons scarcely any traces of them are to be found.

Wilberforce's Practical View, chap. vi.

hearts. Do they speak of the first tabernacle? They call it a 'figure for the time then present. But Christ being come an high priest of good things to come, by His own blood He entered in once into the holy place, having obtained eternal redemption for us.' Do they speak of prophecy? They call the testimony of Jesus the *spirit* of it. Of the gospel? It is Christ crucified. Of the medium by which the world was crucified to them, and they unto the world? It is the cross of Christ. One of the most affecting ideas which they afford us of heaven, consists in ascribing everlasting glory and dominion 'to Him that loved us and washed us from our sins in His own blood.'"[2]

All the lines of evangelical truth meet and centre in Jesus Christ, and therefore He Himself says, "I am the Truth." Were He to be excluded, the several parts of the glorious system would be disconcerted, and the whole frame would be broken in pieces. What would become of the doctrine of redemption, of pardon of sin, of justification, of perseverance, or of future felicity?

Christ Jesus is the life of all the graces and comforts of a Christian in this world. By the knowledge and contemplation of Him, and of His death in our stead, faith lives, and is strengthened from day to day; all the springs of repentance are opened, and flow freely, when the heart is melted by views of a dying Saviour; love feels the attractive power of its glorious object, and is kindled into a holy flame; sin is mortified; the world is subdued; and the hope of future glory is supported, enlivened, and confirmed, so as to become sure and steadfast, like an anchor of the soul. But without Him, whom having not seen we love, these graces would wither and die, or, to speak more properly, they would have no existence.

What is said in the following pages concerning the glory and preciousness of Jesus Christ, is not to be understood as if spoken to the exclusion of the Father, or of the Holy Spirit. But I would

---

2 *Fuller's* Calvinistic and Socinian Systems compared, page 217, 218.

beg leave to say, that I am not able to form any clear, satisfactory, comfortable thoughts of God, suited to awaken my love, or encourage my hope and trust, but as He has been pleased to reveal Himself in the person of Jesus Christ.[3] God was once manifested in the flesh on earth, and He is now manifested in the same human nature in heaven, exercising universal dominion, having the government of heaven, earth, and hell upon His shoulders. "God was in Christ reconciling the world unto Himself." The light of His glory is seen in the face, or person, of Jesus Christ. This is the foundation on which the Christian's hope is built, the fountain whence he derives all his refreshment and consolation.

Till God in human flesh I see,
My thoughts no comfort find;
The holy, just, and sacred Three
Are terrors to the mind.

But if Immanuel's face appear,
My hope, my joy begins;
His name forbids my slavish fear,
His grace removes my sins.

The outlines of our plan, in the ensuing discourse, are: *The character of the persons to whom Christ is precious, The evidence they give that He is precious to them, and In what respects He is so.*

---

3   Jesus Christ says, "I am God, and there is none else." This does not exclude the God-head of the Father. I think it is sufficiently evident from many places of Scripture, that the Father and the Son have an inconceivable communion, and that one and the same Divine nature, which is in the Father, dwells in the Son. For, since divine names and attributes, works and worship, are ascribed to both, they must both be truly God; and since there is but one true God, they must both have fellowship in the same God-head. Hence there is no other God-head but that which dwells in Christ; that God-head in which He partakes by His being one with the Father. "I and My Father are one. I am in the Father, and the Father is in Me." Therefore the apostle says, "All the fullness of the God-head dwells bodily in Him." – *Dr. Watis*

Chapter Two

The Character Of The Persons To Whom Christ Is Precious— You That Believe.

The import of the term *believe* is plain and easy. In common discourse it is so well understood, that no one is at a loss to determine what is intended by it. Every man knows the meaning of his neighbour, when he hears him say, "I believe the fact which you relate," or "I do not believe the report which I hear concerning you." Now, if the term is understood, when it refers to the common affairs of life, why should we be at uncertainties about the meaning of it, when applied to religious subjects? The sacred writers do not use words in a sense directly contrary to their general acceptation. If they did this, the instructions they are authorized to give us, concerning the momentous affairs of our souls, and of eternity, would be wrapped up in impenetrable obscurity.

Yet we find in the sacred writings, two kinds of believing spoken of, and two sorts of believers described. Some believe for a while, but in time of temptation fall away. Simon the sorcerer is said to have believed, when he was in the gall of bitterness, and the bond of iniquity; when his heart was not right in the sight of God.[4] The apostle James speaks of a kind of faith which answers no valuable purpose, because it is destitute of those works which are the proper fruits of true faith. "Dost thou not know, O vain man, that faith without works, is dead?" Such a faith as this is to be found almost every where, in a country favoured with the light of divine revelation, and the ministry of the gospel. But it is quite inefficacious, since the man who is the subject of it is still a slave to sin, a lover of this present evil world, an enemy to God and goodness, and in the broad way which leads to destruction.

The other kind of believing, spoken of by the inspired writers, especially in the New Testament, is that which has pardon of sin, justification before God, and everlasting life annexed to it. "Ye are not of them that draw back unto perdition, but of them that believe to the saving of the soul." This faith is accompanied with certain qualities which are not connected with the other. Though the nominal and real Christian are both said to believe, and the articles of their creed may, in many respects, be the same, yet their dispositions and characters, are essentially different.

---

4   It is said, "*Simon* himself believed also; but it may be inquired, 'What did he believe?' There is reason to conclude from the proofs which he presently gave of his ignorance and impiety, that he knew little or nothing of the real character of the glorious Redeemer. His belief of what he had heard delivered was but in a very partial way. He believed just in the same manner as *Judas* repented. The repentance of that apostate was but partial; and a repentance merely on account of the dreadful consequences of his sin. *Simon* seems to have been prevailed upon, by the wonderful power discovered in the working of miracles, to believe that he, in whose name they were performed, must be divine. He believed that such a person as Christ existed, and likewise some little concerning what He was, as that He was a Being possessed of great power; but the chief part of the Saviour's excellence, which is revealed in the gospel, and constitutes the very essence of it, was unknown to him. Much the same may be said concerning the faith of the stony-ground hearers of the word.—See *Fuller's* Gospel of Christ worthy of all acceptation, page 19. To this author I am indebted for several hints in the following pages.

Now, the leading truth, which is to be believed, is, that Jesus Christ is the Son of God, and the Saviour of the world. "Peter said, 'Thou art Christ, the Son of the living God.' " That is, Thou art the true Messiah, and by way of eminence, the proper Son of the eternal God, and the fountain of life and happiness to all Thy followers. So the apostle speaks to the Romans, "If thou shalt confess with thy mouth the Lord Jesus, and believe in thine heart, that God hath raised him from the dead, thou shalt be saved." The confession which the Ethiopian eunuch made, in order of baptism, amounted to the same thing; "As they went on their way, they came unto a certain water. And the eunuch said, 'See here is water, what doth hinder me to be baptized?' And Philip said, 'If thou believest with all thine heart, thou mayest.' And he answered and said, 'I believe that Jesus Christ is the Son of God.' "

To believe this, is to believe the gospel; for the sum of the gospel is, "that God was in Christ reconciling the world unto Himself, not imputing their trespasses unto them." Or in other words, that the supreme Governor of the world, of His free mercy, for the alone sake of that His Son Jesus Christ has done and suffered, pardons, justifies, and saves the believing sinner. But nothing is more certain, than that a mere nominal Christian, a man who has a name to live, and still is dead in trespasses and sins, may give his assent to all that is expressed above. He may state the articles of an orthodox creed as correctly, in many respects, as any other person. And therefore it is necessary to pay strict attention to those things which accompany true faith, and distinguish it from that which a man may possess, and yet die in his sins.

1. True faith implies that divine illumination whereby we are taught to know ourselves, to know the only true God, and Jesus Christ whom He hath sent, whom to know is life eternal. Faith cannot exist without knowledge; for how is it possible for a man to believe that which he does not understand? Believing in Jesus

Christ to the saving of the soul is the effect of Divine teaching. "It is written in the prophets," said Jesus, "They shall be all taught of God; every one therefore that hath heard, and learned of the Father, cometh unto Me." When Peter made that confession before recited, his Divine Master pronounced him blessed, as being the subject of illumination from above. "Blessed art thou, Simon Barjona; for flesh and blood hath not revealed it unto thee, but My Father, who is in heaven." They that believe are therefore said to know the truth. And thus the apostle Paul tells us, that he "knew whom he had believed."

2. True faith is grounded on the testimony of God. What other idea of faith can we have, than that of believing something revealed, or made known? Hence the prophet says, "Who hath believed our report?" The faith of a Christian is, a divine conviction of the truth of what God hath spoken.

Has the author of our being revealed in His blessed word, the purity of His own nature, His abhorrence of sin, the strictness and holiness of that law by which we are governed? This is known and believed, when, under the illumination of the Divine Spirit, the commandment comes home to the conscience; then sin revives, the awakened sinner gives up his delusive hope, and, in that sense, dies. Has God revealed the depravity of human nature? That the heart of man is deceitful above all things, and desperately wicked; that we are altogether become filthy; that there is none that doeth good, no not one; that we are alienated from the life of God, that we are the servants of sin, the slaves of Satan, children of wrath, under the curse, condemned already, and liable to eternal destruction and misery? All this is in some measure known, and really believed by Him that has true faith.

No man is solicitous about being saved who does not see and feel himself lost. The whole do not apply to the physician, but they who are sick. No man comes to Christ for pardon, who does not see the greatness and grievousness of his sins. No man believes with the heart unto righteousness, who is not convinced of the insufficiency of his own works to justify him before God. No man looks to the Redeemer for justification, who does not see that he is under the sentence of condemnation. No man comes to Jesus that he may have life, who is not sensible, that, as a sinner, he is doomed to death. Thus, faith implies a conviction and belief of what the word of God reveals, concerning the state and condition of fallen man.

Does the divine word reveal a Saviour? Does it inform us, that the Son of God took upon Him our nature, stood in our place, bore our sins, satisfied justice for offences, and reconciled us to God? Does the Father declare unto us, that He is well pleased in His Son, who has obtained eternal redemption for us? This is understood and believed by him that has true faith.

Does the gospel contain promises of pardon, of righteousness, of life and salvation, made to the most wretched and guilty of mankind, who are enabled to come to Jesus for them? Does it assure us, that none are cast out in any wise, or on any account whatsoever, who come unto Him? Faith is no other thing than a sincere and hearty belief of this. It is a divine persuasion of the truth of what the word of God makes known for our belief. Hence it is called "the belief of the truth."

Perhaps there cannot be a better definition of true faith in a few words, than that just mentioned, "the belief of the truth;" and yet it is necessary to inquire what is meant by truth. That Jesus Christ has appeared and sojourned on earth, according to what was predicted of Him; that He was born of a virgin, in the town of Bethlehem; that He preached the gospel, and wrought miracles; that He suffered, was crucified, rose again from the dead, satisfied ascended up into glory, having atoned for sin, satisfied Divine justice, and obtained eternal redemption for us; all this is truth;

but it is not the whole truth. The infinite excellency of the blessed God; the equity, reasonableness, and goodness of His law; the exceeding sinfulness of sin; the ruinous and lost condition of man, as in a state of alienation from his Maker; the absolute need of holiness and purity of heart, in order to final happiness: the infinite loveliness and preciousness of Jesus Christ, and the suitableness and glory of the way of salvation by Him, as in every respect honourable to God, and safe for man; these are branches of the truth which must be believed as firmly as those above mentioned. But they have not full possession of the minds of any, excepting those whose faith is of the operation of God.

They whose hearts are not purified by faith, do not conceive of divine objects as they are in themselves; and therefore they do not believe the truth concerning them. "Thou thoughtest that I was altogether such a one as thyself; but I will reprove thee."

The word of inspiration represents God in His true character; it represents men as they really are; it declares the truth concerning the evil of sin, and its just demerit; it sets forth not only the reality but the excellency of heavenly things. That is, it holds them forth as they are in themselves; and that must undoubtedly be the truth concerning them. To conceive of them otherwise than according to this representation, is not to believe the truth, but to believe a lie. Our blessed Redeemer tells us, that He came to "bear witness to the truth," that is, among other things, to the purity and inflexibility of the law, to the justice and holiness of God, to the evil and demerit of sin, and to the reality of His being the only begotten of the Father, and the Saviour of men. This was to bear witness of things as they really are in themselves. It must therefore be the truth; and a hearty reception and persuasion of it, as it is revealed, is what the apostle calls "the belief of the truth." Thus when he denominates the Thessalonians believers, he immediately signifies what it was which constituted them such, "Because our testimony among you was believed." This testimony is elsewhere called "the testimony of God concerning His Son Jesus Christ." It is that in which the everlasting interests of men are deeply and intimately concerned. "He that hath received this testimony, hath set to his seal that God is true."

3. Faith is the result of serious and impartial inquiry, and of a reverential regard to the authority of God, in what He hath spoken. "The word is nigh thee, even in thy mouth, and in thy heart; that is, the word of faith which we preach; for faith cometh by hearing, and hearing by the word of God." The truth is believed, not from common report, not from the testimony of man, but from the testimony of God. Hence, says the apostle to the Thessalonians, "For this cause we thank God without ceasing, because, when ye received the word of God, which ye heard of us, ye received it not as the word of men, but, as it is in truth, the word of God, which effectually worketh also in you that believe."

4. True faith in Jesus Christ is accompanied with a sincere and hearty approbation of Him, as the alone, the all-sufficient Saviour. It is not a faint, feeble, wavering assent, but such a firm persuasion as, in some measure, corresponds with the strength and clearness of the evidence with which the truth is confirmed. The whole soul acquiesces in the relief which it brings, and approves of the method of salvation which it reveals. There is great propriety in such expressions as these concerning true faith. "If thou believest with all thine heart; With the heart man believeth unto righteousness, and with the mouth confession is made unto salvation." These terms must imply the consent of the judgment, connected with the approbation and acceptance of the will, and the affections. This is faith unfeigned.

Persons may profess to believe this and the other thing, when, in fact, it is but a mere pretence, as is evident from the general tenor of their actions. He who really believes that certain substances are of a poisonous quality will act accordingly; he will carefully avoid them. He who is fully persuaded that fire will burn, cannot be induced to rush into the flames. He who believes that the profits, the pleasures, and the honours of the world will make him happy when he can enjoy them, acts in a manner consistent with what he believes; he pursues these objects with all his might. His belief in this case is not feigned, but real, as is evident by his practice. He who certainly believes that a large estate is left him by a deceased relation, will not delay to put in his claim for it. In all these cases, and many others which daily occur in common life, we see that a real and sincere belief is followed by a corresponding practice.

Apply this to religious subjects. A man professes and pretends to believe, that God is angry with the wicked every day, and that His wrath is revealed from heaven against all ungodliness and unrighteousness of men; yet he lives as unconcerned as if there were no danger; he flees not from the wrath to come; he takes no measures for his soul's escape. Is this man's belief real and hearty, or only a mere pretence? Is it not evident that he does not credit the awful declarations of God's Word with his whole heart?[5]

Another man pretends to believe that sin is the greatest and worst of evils; that there is nothing so odious, nothing so dangerous to the soul, nothing so ruinous and destructive as sin; and yet

5   Justin Martyr, in his apology for the Christians, addressed to the emperor Antoninus Pius, expresses himself to the following purpose: "I must tell you, that of all men living we are the greatest promoters of peace, by teaching, that it is impossible for any worker of iniquity, any covetous or insidious person, to hide himself from God; and that every one is stepping forward to eternal misery or happiness, his works giving evidence for him or against him before the Judge of all." He then adds, "If men were once fully persuaded of these things, (or did they believe them with their whole hearts) who would make the bold adventure to embrace the pleasures of sin for a season, with his eye upon eternal fire at the end of the enjoyment? Who would not strive to the utmost of his power to check himself on the brink of ruin, and seek to be possessed of what is necessary to secure him from everlasting vengeance?" —Justin Martyr, Apol. pro. Christ. xii.

this man secretly loves it, and daily lives in the known and allowed practice of it. What shall we think of his faith in this particular? Is he hearty in his belief? Or rather, since it has had no influence on his life and walk, is it not a mere pretence?

Others again profess to believe that there is a real excellency in religion; that wisdom's ways are lovely, pleasant and peaceful; and that no joy can be compared with that of serving and pleasing God; and yet they live in the continual neglect of every thing they pretend to approve. Can a faith so utterly inefficacious be real and sincere? Is it thus that men believe with the heart unto righteousness? Surely not.

Do such persons tell us that they believe in the Lord Jesus Christ, and declare that there is no object so desirable, so excellent, so lovely as He is in their estimation? While at the same time, the world has full possession of their hearts, they mind earthly things, and are entire strangers to a conversation in heaven. Surely such a faith is but imaginary; for unfeigned faith "worketh by love" to its object.

5. In true faith there is a deep conviction of the importance of what is believed. It is far from being considered as a trifling, uninteresting concern. It is viewed as the most interesting of any thing that can possibly engage the attention of mankind; as what relates to the life of the soul, and to its everlasting state. He that believes is like a man whose house is on fire, and who is eager to have it saved from the devouring flames. Or like a shipwrecked mariner, struggling amidst the overwhelming billows of the deep, but beholding before him a rock whereupon he may rest with safety.

Those who talk of their faith in Christ, and at the same time have little or no abiding concern about the salvation of their souls, and the affairs of a future world, do but deceive themselves. They who believe are compared in the Scriptures to the man-slayer, who, sensible of his danger from the avenger of blood, ran with all his might to the city appointed for the protection of such persons. "Ye have fled for refuge, to lay hold on the hope set before you." What the angel said to *Lot*, when he brought him out of Sodom, may be applied to him who is warned to flee from the wrath to come; "Escape for thy life, look not behind thee, neither stay thou in all the plain; escape to the mountain lest thou be consumed." When the jailor at Philippi was awakened to a just sense of his guilty and ruined condition, in an agony of distress he inquired, whether there were any possible way of relief for him, "Sirs, what must I do to be saved? And they said, Believe in the Lord Jesus Christ, and thou shalt be saved."

Such is the description which our Lord Jesus Christ Himself gives of faith in His name. "As Moses lifted up the serpent in the wilderness, so must the Son of man be lifted up; that whosoever believeth in Him should not perish, but have everlasting life." The allusion is to what God said to Moses, "Make thee a fiery serpent, and set it upon a pole; and it shall come to pass, that every one that is bitten, when he looketh upon it, shall live." Here a divine remedy was provided against a national calamity; a sovereign antidote against spreading and mortal poison. Those who were stung and perishing, though they were at the utmost limits of the camp, might look up to the brazen serpent and find health and life.

Physicians were of no use in that dreadful malady; human efforts, applications, plasters, or medicines were insignificant. The swift and fiery poison operated powerfully in such as were bitten, and, without relief, they were quickly brought to the very borders of the grave. But though they were just about to expire, if they could but cast a look towards the appointed remedy, they were sure of healing and recovery. On the confines of the grave, and the brink of death, they were restored to life and happiness, by a look to the brazen image of the serpent. A most lively picture this of a believing sinner. He is in himself as one ready to perish, but being enabled to believe the promises of grace in Jesus Christ, and looking to Him that he may be saved, he is pardoned and healed; he is delivered from going down to the pit, through the ransom which has been found and accepted for him, and his life shall see the light: or, according to the words of our blessed Redeemer Himself, "He shall not perish, but have everlasting life."

6. True faith is connected with repentance of sin. If we are not turned from sin to God, if sin is not made bitter to us, if it does not appear hateful, if our hearts are not penetrated with sorrow, grief, and self-abhorrence on account of it, in vain do we imagine ourselves to be believers in Jesus. Looking unto Him whom we have pierced, is accompanied with mourning and bitterness of soul. That faith which leaves the heart impenitent, is not saving; for repentance is absolutely necessary to salvation. Our blessed Redeemer said to a certain woman in the gospel, "Thy faith hath saved thee, go in peace." But what was the attendant of the faith she possessed? Was it not penitence? She wept at the feet of Jesus, she washed His feet with her tears, and wiped them with the hair of her head. She remembered her own evil ways, and her doings which were not good, and loathed herself in her own sight. Repentance and faith are inseparably united; the one perhaps never exists in the mind of a sinner without the other. If we have ever beheld Jesus with sincere delight, as a Saviour from sin, we shall mourn heartily that ever we sinned against Him. We cannot but repent of sin, while we look for the forgiveness of it, through His astonishing love in dying for us, that so He might deliver us from eternal destruction. Repentance is justly said by some, to be the tear of love dropping from the eye of faith.

7. True faith in Jesus Christ is attended with subjection of heart and life to His will and government. For by faith the heart is purified, and consequently the life. To believe the gospel is to obey from the heart that form of doctrine which was delivered unto us.

Faith worketh by love, both to God and man; and therefore it is positively affirmed, that "faith without works is dead." Talk not of your faith in Jesus, if you have no love to His dear name. Pretend not to love Him, if you are not concerned to please Him. "This is the love of God, that we keep His commandments; and His commandments are not grievous." Our Divine Saviour Himself says, "He that hath My commandments, and keepeth them, he it is that loveth Me." The works of a real Christian are not the production of a spirit of legality; they are works of faith and labours of love, which are shewn to His name. Such is the efficacy of a lively faith, that it is the vigorous root to all holy obedience; it bears up the soul amidst the severest trials; it strengthens it for the most arduous services; enables it to overcome the world, and to lay hold upon eternal life. By way of describing its efficacy, I shall beg leave to make a short extract from a very ancient Christain writer.

Justin Martyr, describing the worship and the practice of believers, in his apology for the primitive Christians, says, "We worship the Creator of the universe, not with blood, libations and incense, of which we are sufficiently taught, He stands in no need; but we exalt Him to the best of our power, with the rational service of prayers and praises, in all the oblations we make to Him; believing this to be the only honour worthy of Him. We approve ourselves thankful to Him, and express our gratitude in the most solemn hymns, for our creation, our preservation, the various blessings of His providence, and the hopes of a resurrection to a life incorruptible, which we are sure to have for asking, if we ask in faith. 'Who, that knows any thing of us, will not confess this to be our way of worshipping? The Master, who instructed us in this kind of worship, and who was born for this purpose, and crucified under Pontius Pilate, procurator of Judea, in the reign of Tiberius Caesar, is Jesus Christ whom we believe to be the Son of the true God.

"We who were formerly guilty of impure practices, now strictly keep ourselves within the bounds of chastity. We, who devoted ourselves to magic arts, now consecrate ourselves entirely to the true God. We, who loved nothing so much as our possessions, now produce all we have in common, and spread our whole stock before our indigent brethren. We, who were instigated with hatred to one another, and would not so much as warm ourselves at the same fire with those of a different tribe, now live and diet together, praying sincerely for our enemies. All our return for evils are but the gentlest persuasives to convert those who unjustly hate us, that they, being brought to a conformity to Christ, might be filled with the same comfortable hopes of enjoying the like happiness with ourselves. Christ commands His disciples to shine with a distinguishing patience and meekness, and to win men over from their sins, by such gentle methods of conversion.

"I could give you a proof of the influence of such bright examples from many converts among us, who, from men of violence and oppression, were transformed into quite another nature, perfectly overcome by the passive courage of their Christian neighbours, or by observing the astonishing patience of such injured Christians as have fallen under their notice, or, lastly, by the experience they have had of the fidelity of such persons in their dealings."[6]

In another place this ancient apologist says, "Those who do not make the precepts of Christ the rule of their lives, are to be looked upon as no Christians, let them say ever such fine things of His law. Those who are believers or Christians in word only, who talk of religion, but do not practice it, if such smart for their hypocrisy, it is no more than they deserve. Jesus Himself hath said, 'Every tree that bringeth not forth good fruit, is hewn down and cast into the fire. Not every one that saith unto Me, Lord, Lord,

---

6   *Justin Martyr*, Apol. Pro. Christ. xviii, &c.

shall enter into the kingdom of heaven; but he that doeth the will of My Father who is in heaven.' "

"I shall now," says he, "lay before you the manner of our dedicating ourselves to God, upon our conversion; for should I omit this, I might seem not to deal sincerely in this account of the Christian religion. As many therefore as are *persuaded*, and *believe* that the things taught by us are true, and are determined to live accordingly, are taught to pray with fasting, and to ask of God the forgiveness of their former sins, we also praying and fasting together with them; they are then, and not till then, brought to a place of water, and baptized,[7] after the same manner as ourselves have been; for they are washed in the name of God the Father, and Lord of all, and of our Saviour Jesus Christ. This baptism is called illumination, because the minds of the catechumens, who are thus washed, are illuminated. And, moreover, the person baptized and illuminated is baptized in the name of the Holy Ghost, who spake by the prophets, and foretold every thing concerning Christ."

"After the believer is baptized," says the ancient writer, "and incorporated, or made one with us, we lead him to the congregation of the brethren, as we call them, and then with great fervency pour out our souls in prayer, both for ourselves, for the person baptized, and for all others throughout the whole world; that, having embraced the truth, our conversation may be as becometh the gospel, and that we, being found doers of the word, may at length be saved with an everlasting salvation."[8] Such is the testimony given by this very respectable advocate for the Christian cause.

True faith transforms the temper and frame of our souls into another image, even the image of Christ. This is done, in some degree, in the first saving discovery which we have of Him; so

---

7   Those writers, commonly called The Fathers, frequently though improperly express baptism by regeneration.

8   *Just. Martyr*, Apol. Pro. Christ. xviii, &c.

that he who believes in Jesus is a new creature. Compare the two following passages together; in the former, the apostle says, "Neither circumcision availeth any thing, nor uncircumcision, but faith which worketh by love;" in the letter, "Neither circumcision availeth any thing, nor uncircumcision, but a new creature." We hence infer, that to be a real believer is to be a new creature. "Beholding as in a glass the glory of the Lord, we are changed into the same image from glory to glory, even as by the Spirit of the Lord." Our very tempers are changed into His holy likeness; the meek and lowly, the devout and heavenly mind, which was in Christ Jesus, in some degree, takes place in us.

Faith happily influences all the powers of the soul, and all the actions of the life, according to the degree of its vigour, strength, and liveliness. The more we live by faith on Jesus, the more steadily we look to Him, and the more we shall be transformed into His likeness. We lay aside every weight, and the sin that easily besets us; we run the race which is set before us, looking unto Jesus. As the face of Moses shone when he had seen the Divine glory, so there will be some rays of holiness in our conversation in the world, if we live by faith in the Son of God.

8. True faith sets all things in a different light before the eyes of the soul, and gives it quite another view of them. "It is," says Dr. Watts, "like some heavenly glass applied to the organ of sense, which not only assists and improves our sight, but represents all things in a divine light, even such as they appear to the blessed spirits above. It alters the view and appearance of all the great and gay things of this life. The treasures, the splendour, and the entertainments of this world, were once the most inviting objects upon which we could look; but now we look on the world, with all the gayest and the richest scenes of it, as little, mean, and despicable things. We are crucified to the world by the cross of Christ. We seek the things which are above, where our Redeemer sitteth at

the right hand of God; and when the world begins to flatter us again, and to appear great and tempting in our eyes, renewed discoveries of His glory, who is the chief among ten thousand, and altogether lovely, eclipse the splendour of all below the skies. 'This is the victory that overcometh the world, even our faith.' "

The awful attributes of God, His holiness, His righteousness and justice were once the terror of our souls; so that we turned our eyes away, and could not contemplate Him with pleasure. As we had no solid hope in His mercy or His love, we saw nothing in Him desirable or delightful to us. We stood afar off from Him; we neglected and forgot Him; or, perhaps, like our first parents, we vainly endeavoured to hide ourselves from Him. The awful threatenings of His displeasure were to us as the messengers of damnation. We beheld them as so many angels with flaming swords, to forbid our entrance into Paradise. But now, being enabled to believe in Jesus, who delivers us from the wrath to come, the terrors of the law have no more such a dreadful aspect. We know that the sword of justice has awoke against the man who was God's fellow, and that all its vengeance was executed upon Him, as our surety. The threatenings of the Almighty are therefore now disarmed, and no longer stand as barriers in the way, to forbid our happiness.

The law proclaims no terror now,
And Sinai's thunder roars no more.

We behold God in Christ, as reconciling sinners unto Himself, not imputing their trespasses unto them. Hence we are enabled to look upon Him in His whole character, not only without dismay, but with a measure of delight. We "give thanks at the remembrance of His holiness;" we survey and dwell upon His glories with awful pleasure; we lift up our eyes towards Him with humble confidence, as our reconciled God, our Father and our Friend for ever.

Our consciences were burdened with guilt. We said unto the Most High, "Our flesh trembleth for fear of Thee, and we are afraid of Thy judgment." We could find no relief till we were led to the cross of the bleeding Prince of peace. He who hung upon the tree took off our burdens, sprinkled us with His own blood, undertook to secure us effectually from Divine wrath, and said unto us, "Fear not, I have redeemed you; your sins are forgiven you; go in peace.

We believe that His blood is sufficient to atone for our offence, and procure us pardon; that His righteousness is sufficient for our acceptance unto eternal life; that His power and grace are sufficient to conquer all our sins, to deliver us out of temptations, to sanctify our vitiated appetites and passions, to incline our wills to holiness, to strengthen us for the performance of good works, to accomplish in us all the good pleasure of His goodness, and the work of faith with power.

9. The believing which is spoken of in the passage under consideration, endears Christ to the soul; since it is said, He is precious to them that so believe. It enthrones Him in the heart; for He dwells in the hearts of His people by faith. The proof of this is attempted in the following pages.

10. In a word, true faith is attended with a measure of solid peace and divine joy. These are experienced in different degrees by believers in Jesus, according to the strength or weakness of their faith. But we are assured, that in the Lord all the seed of Israel shall not only be justified, but they shall glory. This they do in an especial manner, when they are filled with all joy and peace in believing, and made to abound in hope through the power of the Holy Ghost. True faith fixes on that which alone can give peace and rest to the mind, the atoning blood and perfect righteousness of our Lord Jesus Christ. "We joy in God through Jesus Christ our Lord, by whom we have now received the atonement."

The happiness of a believer's life consists in having his mind stayed on the all-sufficient Redeemer by way of fervent affections, lively hope, and steady confidence; for "Thou wilt keep him in perfect peace," says the prophet, "whose mind is stayed on Thee, because he trusteth in Thee." The apostle Peter, writing to a scattered, dispersed, persecuted people, concerning Jesus, says, "Whom having not seen ye love; in whom, though now ye see Him not, yet believing, ye rejoice with joy unspeakable and full of glory."

It may easily be inferred from what has been said, as well as from many passages of Scripture, that the faith of a true Christian is not the mere effort of nature and reason, but the gift of God. It is therefore called the faith of the operation of God. If we savingly believe the truth of the gospel, and its glorious promises, it is "given us so to believe, according to the working of God's mighty power, which He wrought in Christ when He raised Him from the dead."

It may be allowed, as a late writer observes, that believing, simply considered, is a natural act of the mind; but believing such things as the gospel reveals, and understanding the nature and excellency of them, must be a spiritual act. To think, and to love, simply considered, are natural acts; but to think good thoughts, and to love holiness, are spiritual acts. The faith which is attended with such powerful effects, as have been mentioned, is not of ourselves; but is one of those good and perfect gifts which come down from the Father of lights, with whom is no variableness, nor shadow of turning. However strong, rational, or convincing the evidence may be which accompanies the testimony of God, yet without the operation of His blessed Spirit, it will not effectually subdue the mind which is blinded by prejudice, bloated with pride, benumbed with carelessness, and poisoned with enmity against the truth.

We describe the operations of a gracious mind in detail, as if a considerable space of time were requisite for the production of them; but it ought to be remembered, that the change wrought in a sinner's conceptions and views, in his transformations from death unto life, from a state of nature to a state of grace, may be instantaneous. For there is no middle condition between death and life, enmity and reconciliation, unbelief and faith, or condemnation and justification. The publican, oppressed with conscious guilt, cried out, as he smote upon his breast, "God be merciful to me a sinner," and he went down to his house justified. The jailor at Philippi inquired what he must do to be saved, and the same night gave evidence of an entire change of mind; for it is said, "he believed, rejoicing in God with all his house." The Lord opened the heart of Lydia, and she attended to the things which were spoken of Paul. Three thousand of Peter's hearers, on the day of Pentecost, hardened in impenitence, and fixed in unbelief, were at once pricked in their hearts, under awful apprehensions of their sin and danger; they were directed to the Divine remedy provided for the relief of ruined man, they gladly received the word, were baptized, and the same day added to the church. The conversion of Zacchaeus was somewhat similar. It is true, all these were extraordinary instances of the power of saving grace. But in all other cases, I humbly apprehend, the change, as it is in itself, and as it is in the sight of God, must be instantaneous, though the discovery of it, both to the sinner's own satisfaction, and to the satisfaction of others, is often very gradual. The precise period when it takes place is known to God, though it is often unknown to the party himself, otherwise than by the effects which follow upon it.

The entrance of God's word giveth light; but the light at first is not clear and distinct. The God that caused the light to shine out of darkness, shineth into the sinner's benighted heart, to give the light of the knowledge of His glory in the face of Jesus Christ. Yet it is but a very little which any believer knows at first, in comparison with the discoveries which are afterwards made to him. Perhaps all he can say bears some resemblance to the language of the young man in the gospel, who had been born blind, "One thing I know, that whereas I was blind, now I see." Faith, in like manner, may be at first but as a grain of mustardseed, but it is a great happiness when "your faith groweth exceedingly, and," as its proper attendant, when "your charity towards each other aboundeth." The disciples said unto the Lord, "Increase our faith."[9]

The great things which are ascribed to faith by the inspired writers, should induce us to be very deeply concerned to be partakers of it. We find them constantly asserting such things concerning faith as may convince us of its great use. Men have remission of sins through faith; they are justified by faith; their hearts are purified by faith; they have access to God by faith; they live, they walk, they stand by faith; they overcome all enemies by faith; they are kept by the power of God through faith, and, to comprehend all in one word, they are saved by faith. How necessary, how important then is the apostle's exhortation, "Examine yourselves whether ye be in the faith!"

Faith, we see, is neither more nor less than a cordial belief of the truth. So the divine word defines it. "These things were written that ye might believe that Jesus is the Christ, the Son of God,

---

9   It is not necessary that all these several workings of the heart should be plain, distinct, and sensible in every true believer. For the actions of the soul, and especially the springs, the motives, and designs of those actions, are so hidden, and so mingled with each other, that they are not all distinctly perceived, even by the man himself in whom they take place. When the poor man in the gospel said, "Lord I believe; help Thou my unbelief," there were a multitude of crowding thoughts and passions, which produced and mingled with those ideas and expressions of fear and faith, that could never be distinctly apprehended and recounted by the person who felt them.—*Dr. Watts.*

Yet the concomitants of saving faith, or those things which prove it to be such, should be carefully attended to, lest we should deceive ourselves in a matter of so much importance.

and that, believing, ye might have life through His name." But then it may be said of faith as of love to God, of desire after Him, and of hope and joy in Him, by their fruits ye shall know them. They are all distinguished and discerned to be true and genuine, by their attendants, and the way in which they are manifested.

In respect to faith, the word of God fully and clearly sets before us what are its attendants and its fruits, where it is true and unfeigned. It is the less needful to enlarge on them here, because this is intended to be done through the whole of the following chapter. I hope the brief and simple account of faith, already given, will not be found materially defective. And I would earnestly entreat the reader to examine Himself concerning this important article. No subject of a religious nature is perhaps more controverted than this. But after all that has been said upon it, on one side and another, I apprehend it is evident from the Scriptures.

That no man is a true believer whose heart is not changed by the grace and Spirit of God. "For if any man be in Christ he is a new creature; old things are passed away; behold all things are become new." "Being dead in your sins, ye are risen with Him, through the faith of the operation of God." The faith of him who lives a careless, unconcerned, thoughtless life, is vain; he is yet in his sins.

No man is a true believer, in whom the blessed Spirit of God does not dwell, as his teacher and guide. "As many as are led by the Spirit of God, they are the sons of God; but if any man have not the Spirit of Christ, he is none of His." "When He, the Spirit of truth, is come, He shall guide you into all truth. He shall reprove the world of sin, of righteousness, and of judgment. He shall glorify me, for He shall take of mine, and shall shew it unto you." The man who has never had a heart-affecting discovery of the purity of God's law, of the exceeding sinfulness and just demerit of sin, of his own guilty and depraved condition, of his utter helplessness, and the insufficiency of any righteousness he can perform, to recommend him to the Divine favour; the man who has never been taught, in an efficacious way, the glory of Christ's person, the sufficiency of His sacrifice, as a proper atonement for sin, the perfections of His righteousness, the fulness of His grace, and His ability to save to the uttermost: the man who has not been taught these things, in some degree, is yet in a state of unbelief. How can he have faith who knows not what God's Word reveals as the truth? "I know," says the apostle, "whom I have believed."

He is no true believer whose heart is not attached to Jesus Christ above all; who sees no beauty, no excellency, no loveliness in Him; for to all those who believe He is precious. When the apostle Paul requires us to examine ourselves, whether we be in the faith, he adds, "Know ye not your ownselves, how that Jesus Christ is in you, except ye be reprobates?" According to him, to be in the faith, and to have Christ dwelling in us, so as to possess the chief place in our affections, and bear away in our souls, are one and the same thing.

He is no true believer, in whom the Word of God does not dwell, in its sanctifying power and energy. Where the truth is cordially believed, it enters the mind, it is received into the heart, it is incorporated with the soul, and it dwells and abides there. "The truth dwelleth in you. My word abideth in you. It worketh effectually in you that believe. It is in you as the ingrafted word which is able to save the soul. Ye have obeyed from the heart that form of doctrine which was delivered unto you." All these emphatical expressions are descriptive of them that believe. Hence is that remarkable account of faith which is given us by the apostle to the Hebrews, where he tells us, that "faith is the substance of things hoped for." It realizes them, and gives them a subsistence in the mind and heart. The law of God is written there. The truth of

Christ abides there, in its light, its energy, its sanctifying and governing power. It bears sway in the soul, and rules the life. Reader, this is faith unfeigned, faith in reality, or as the apostle Peter terms it, "precious faith;" precious in its author, its object, its use, its efficacy, and its end.

It must appear to every attentive reader, from what has been said, that the Lord Jesus Christ, in His work of mediation for the recovery and salvation of lost sinners, as proposed in the promises of the gospel, is the proper object of faith. Hence it is called a believing in Him, and a believing on His name. If men would attend to their own experience in the applications they make to God for pardon and salvation, many unnecessary disputes concerning faith would be prevented. Every true Christian knows, that he has been enabled, with his whole heart, to believe the divine promises, containing and proposing the atonement of the Redeemer, as the procuring cause of our reconciliation and peace with God, according to the riches of His infinite grace and mercy. "To Him give all the prophets witness, that through His name, whosoever believeth in Him, shall receive remission of sins." Every Christian knows, that he has sincerely approved, and does still heartily approve of the way of justification and salvation by Jesus Christ, proposed in the gospel, as affording a most glorious display of the wisdom, the holiness, the love, and the mercy of God. Hence the apostle Paul describes the faith of those who are called, by its approbation of the wisdom and power of God in the plan of salvation. "We preach Christ crucified unto the Jews a stumbling-block, and unto the Greeks foolishness; but unto them that are called, both Jews and Greeks, Christ the power of God, and the wisdom of God." In the want of this gracious acquiescence in the gospel scheme, consists the nature of unbelief. Without this, no man is influenced by evangelical motives, to hate and renounce sin, or to devote himself to God in the way of obedience. But wherever this cordial sincere approbation of the way of life by Jesus Christ doth prevail in the mind, it will certainly produce humiliation for sin, and holiness of life.

The immediate design of Jehovah, in the great and important concern of our salvation, is, to display His own infinite perfections; "to declare His righteousness, to commend His love, to manifest His wisdom and His power," as His Word every where testifies; and the business of faith, in receiving the ineffable benefits of His salvation, is to give that glory to Him which He designs so to exalt. Abraham, being strong in the faith, gave glory to God; and this is the nature of faith, even in its weakest degree. "We behold His glory, as in a glass. He gives us the light of the knowledge of His glory, in the face of Jesus Christ." The soul of a believer doth herein give unto God, the glory of all those holy properties of His nature, which He designed to manifest, in our salvation by His own dear Son. To Him the Father said, "Thou art My servant, O Israel, in whom I will be glorified." And He directs us to fix our believing regards on Him as such: "Behold My servant, whom I uphold, mine Elect, in whom My soul delighteth; I have put My Spirit upon Him; He shall bring forth judgment unto the Gentiles."

Before I conclude this chapter, I would beg leave, in a plain and serious manner, to address those who are yet in a state of impenitence and unbelief. Supposing you then, my dear reader, to be in this condition, I would entreat you, by all that regard which you ought to have for the everlasting welfare and salvation of your own soul, to consider what the blessed God says to you in His holy word, that word according to which you are to be judged at the last day.

The gospel, as we have seen, plainly declares, that God has contrived a way for the reconciling of sinners unto Himself; that His was accomplished by His substituting His own, His only begotten Son, in the room of the guilty, sending Him into the world to work out salvation for them, delivering Him up to death, even the death of the cross, as an atoning sacrifice for their offences, and raising Him again from the dead for their justification. It declares, that, by this divine expedient, the law which they had violated is perfectly fulfilled and magnified, Divine justice fully satisfied, and God well pleased and glorified. It also declares, that whosoever heartily receives and believes this testimony, upon the authority of Him who reveals it, shall most certainly be saved; and that purely by free grace; without any respect to works or merits of His own, through the redemption which is in Jesus Christ.

Upon this ground the gospel addresses sinners as such, sinners of every rank and degree, calling upon them to regard and believe its gracious messages, that they may be saved. It not only contains a declaration of facts, concerning the person and work of the Redeemer, but the kindest invitations and exhortations, founded upon that declaration. The Son of God Himself represents the preaching of the gospel, under the notion of inviting to a marriage supper, where all things are prepared and ready for the guests. All sorts of persons are invited; the poor, the maimed, the halt, and the blind; they are called from all those places which may be supposed to be haunts of the destitute and the miserable; such as the streets and lanes of the city, and the highways and hedges of the country. The servants are commanded to bid these sons and daughters of want and wretchedness to come to the marriage; nay, even by those efforts of persuasion, which are mighty through God, to *compel* them to come in, that the wedding may be furnished with guests.

What Jesus Christ represents by way of parable, the apostle Paul holds forth without a figure. Attend to what he says with the greatest closeness, my dear reader; it is not a vain thing; your life is in it: "All things are of God, who hath reconciled us to Himself by

Jesus Christ, and hath given to us the ministry of reconciliation, to wit, That God was in Christ reconciling the world unto Himself, not inputing their trespasses unto them; and hath committed unto us the word of reconciliation. Now then, we are ambassadors for Christ, as though God did beseech you by us, we pray you, in Christ's stead, be ye reconciled to God." These ambassadors were to press home the doctrine of reconciliation upon guilty, rebellious men, as the grand motive and argument, through the power of Divine grace, to engage them to give up themselves to God, to acquaint themselves with Him, and so to be at peace. This is the drift and scope, not of a few passages only, but of the whole of the New Testament. That this may not pass unnoticed, the Author of that divine book says, in the conclusion of it, "I am the Root and the offspring of David, the bright and the Morning-star; and the Spirit and the Bride say, Come; and let him that heareth, say, Come; and let him that is athirst come; and whosoever will, let him take the water of life freely." Language more kind, more generous or more free, cannot possibly be devised. Yet this is perfectly conformable to what Jesus said to sinners, when He Himself sojourned amongst them: "In the last day, the great day of the feast, Jesus stood and cried, saying, if any man thirst, let him come unto Me and drink. He that believeth on Me, as the Scripture hath said, out of his belly shall flow rivers of living water." Nothing can be plainer, than that this was addressed to those who were then in a state of unbelief: O that you may attend to it, and receive it with thankfulness and joy, giving glory to God for the richness and freeness of His grace.

Let not your own inability to believe in Jesus Christ be considered as an insuperable bar; for He that calls you to this, can, at the same time, give you power. He who spoke the world into existence, He who quickens the dead by His potent word, may, with the greatest propriety, say to him who is dead in trespasses and sins, "Awake, thou that sleepest, arise from the dead, and Christ shall give thee light." His word is quick and powerful. It is as fire to quicken the lifeless soul, and as a hammer, to break the rock in pieces. It shall not return unto Him void, but shall accomplish that which He pleases, and prosper in the thing whereunto He sends it.

Unbelievers are spoken of in the word of God as being dead in sin; by which is intended, their lying under a charge of guilt, which subjects them to condemnation; and their being under the power and dominion of sin. But this moral death is not, in all respects, like the natural death of the body; for then the use of means to quicken and rouse such persons, would not only be improper, but absolutely hopeless. Sinner, you have a conscience, you have a sense of right and wrong, you have hopes, you have fears, and other affections, capable of being wrought upon by those means which God has appointed. Your guilt will therefore be aggravated in proportion to the means of instruction you enjoy, and the warnings and exhortations given you, if you are not brought to repentance. This is so evident from the word of God, that it seems unnecessary to produce particular proofs of it. From this consideration it is plain, that you are capable of instruction, and of conviction, by the use of those means which Divine wisdom has ordained for that purpose; otherwise your guilt would not be heightened by disregarding them.

There is such a suitableness in the means which God has appointed, for bringing you to the knowledge of the truth, that if you should obstinately reject them, you would be entirely without excuse. The gospel is the happy expedient for quickening those who are dead in sin, since it is the power of God to the salvation of every one that believeth. The most wonderful effects are ascribed to it; it enlightens the understanding, it quickens the conscience, it converts the soul, and sanctifies the mind. And though it does not produce these effects, without the agency of the blessed Spirit of God, yet His agency is not to be considered as abstracted from the means; for He works by them on the minds of men, and gives them all their efficacy.

Open that precious book, the New Testament, my dear fellow-sinner, and you will presently find, that the God of infinite mercy invites you to repent, and believe the gospel. At the same time, you will find, that He does not call you to believe, without shewing you what you are to believe, and exhibiting the clearest and fullest evidence for it. Neither does He call you to repent, without declaring unto you, both your sin, and your danger on account of it. I will suppose that you have read this divine book, and that you have repeatedly heard the gospel preached. You are not then in the same state of total ignorance in which you once were. You know something of religion in theory. You have received some information which you once had not, both concerning your danger, and the divine remedy. Give me leave to remind you, that if you should neglect so great salvation, you will be hereby rendered quite inexcusable. For such neglect must now be the effect of perverseness, and not simply of ignorance. But O that your attention may be engaged to the evidence and the importance of the gospel-message; and that your heart may be won to believe and embrace the truth as it is in Jesus! Remember, that the declaration of it is accompanied with the most kind and tender invitations, entreaties and expostulations, which are urged in the Scriptures, by the most alluring and alarming motives that can possibly be proposed to the human mind. God forbid that you should be proof against them all, and harden yourself in unbelief, to your own utter ruin! Give the gospel a fair hearing; consider its evidence; attend to its kind and pathetic entreaties. Search the Scriptures daily, whether these things are so. The Bereans did this, and the sacred historian tells us, that "therefore many of them believed."

Let me entreat you to attempt the solemn work of calling upon God by earnest prayer and supplication. Hearken to what He Himself says unto you, in reference to this: "Seek ye the Lord while He may be found, call ye upon Him while He is near; let the wicked forsake his way, and the unrighteous man his thoughts; and let him return unto the Lord, and He will have mercy upon him; and to our God, for He will abundantly pardon."[10]

The gospel holds forth immediate relief to a wounded conscience. The same hour that the jailor at Philippi asked, "What must I do to be saved?" he was told that the remedy was at hand; "Believe in the Lord Jesus Christ, and thou shalt be saved." No long course of preparation, no pre-requisites, no previous qualifications are necessary. Should they indeed be sought, they would be sought in vain. Humiliation for sin, love to God, devotedness to Him, and victory over sin and the world, are not to be looked for in ourselves, in order that we may, on such grounds, be encouraged to believe; so far from it, that they are spoken of in the Scriptures as the certain *effects* consequent upon believing. The legal spirit of which we are all naturally possessed, leads us to imagine, that we must not embrace the promise of life by Christ Jesus, unless we are some way fitted, prepared and qualified for so doing. This is a perversion of the free proclamation of the gospel, and turning, in some sort, the covenant of grace into a covenant of works. This is setting the gospel remedy at so great a distance, that it is impossible for us to claim the benefit of it. Whereas, "the word is high thee, even in thy mouth, and in thy heart, that is, the word of faith which we preach; that if thou shalt confess with thy mouth the Lord Jesus, and shalt believe in thine heart that God hath raised Him from the dead, thou shalt be saved." The glory of

---

10 See an excellent little piece, entitled *Thoughts on the Calls and Invitations of the Gospel*; printed at Edinburgh, and sold by Guthrie and Ogle, price 6d. I suppose the author to be Mr. M'Lean; but whoever he be, he has my sincerest thanks for this judicious production of his pen.

this inestimable blessing is, that it is absolutely free to sinners, as such, of every rank and degree; and like the brazen serpent to the wounded, dying Israelites, it is designed to give immediate relief to perishing souls. "Whosoever believeth in Him shall not perish. Whosoever will, let him come," without seeking for any kind of recommendation whatever. If he is a sinner, for such the remedy is provided. "This is a faithful saying, and worthy of all acceptation, that Jesus Christ came into the world to save sinners." It is a deplorable mistake to look for the effects of faith where the efficacious cause of those effects is wanting. Does the afflicted person say, "As soon as I am cured of this deadly distemper, I will call in the help of a physician?" The man who is fallen into an horrible pit, whose feet stick fast in the miry clay, wants immediate relief, and never thinks of waiting till he is qualified to deserve it, from the friendly hand which is ready to draw him out. When Peter was sinking in the mighty deep, he instantly cried out, "Lord, save me, or I perish."

They who have believed through grace are, in the word of inspiration, described by those holy dispositions, and that heavenly walk, which are the necessary fruits and appendages of faith; as such, I have endeavoured to point them out in the preceding pages. But it would be a strange perversion of the order of things, to conclude that we must not believe the promises of salvation by Jesus Christ, till we find in ourselves those fruits which can only be experienced in consequence of believing them. Remember, my dear fellow-sinner, that your hearts can only be *purified by faith*, and that love to God, and conformity to His will, follow upon believing, as effects which are dependent on their cause. Let the tree be made good, and its fruit may be expected to be so; but men do not gather grapes of thorns, or figs of thistles. "Without faith it is impossible to please God. This is the work of God," a work most acceptable in His sight, "that ye believe in Him whom He hath sent." The history of Christ, the truths of His gospel, and the promises of His grace, "were written, that ye might believe that Jesus is the Christ, the Son of God, and that believing, ye might have life through His name." Thus the God of all grace proposed to our first parent, in his lost, forlorn, and hopeless condition, the promise of redemption by Christ, the belief of which, no doubt, brought him back from the borders of despair, and gave him immediate relief.

THE AWAKENED SINNER'S ADDRESS TO GOD, SUITED TO THE FOREGOING REMARKS.

Almighty and everlasting God, my Creator, my Preserver, and my Judge, before whose awful tribunal I must shortly make my appearance. I am a poor individual of the fallen race of mankind, shapen in iniquity, conceived in sin, and chargeable with actual transgressions almost without number. I have brought myself under the condemning sentence of Thy righteous law, and rendered myself deserving of Thine everlasting displeasure. It is high time for me to awake out of sleep, and to inquire, with the utmost seriousness, and the deepest concern, whether there be any possible way of escaping that wrath which is revealed from heaven against all ungodliness and unrighteousness of men?

I feel a ray of hope spring up in my soul, since Thou hast said, in Thy holy word, "ye have destroyed yourselves, but in Me is your help." Jesus Christ Thy only begotten Son, came into the world to save sinners, such as I am. This is no delusive supposition, no uncertain report; it is a faithful saying, and worthy of all acceptation. But I learn from the sacred Scriptures, that he who disregards this testimony, who receives it not in the love of the truth, who believes not in the Son of God, the appointed Saviour, must everlastingly perish. I learn from Thy word, that parson of sin deliverance from condemnation, and the enjoyment of eternal felicity, are inseparably connected with true faith in His name.

Do Thou mercifully impart to me that divine illumination, without which I shall neither know the way of peace, nor believe the truth to the saving of my soul. O teach me to know myself, the deep depravity of my nature, the guiltiness of my whole life, the purity of that law which I have violated, the inflexibility of that holiness and justice which I have offended, the exceeding sinfulness of sin, and my own utter inability to do any thing, towards delivering my own soul out of that state of misery into which I have brought myself. Bring me to an acquaintance with Thee, the only true God, and with Jesus Christ, whom Thou hast sent to redeem and save the lost and the undone, whom to know is life eternal. May Thy Holy Spirit set before me, in the most powerful and engaging manner, the glory of His person, the sufficiency of His sacrifice, the efficacy of His blood to cleanse from all sin, the perfection of His righteousness to clothe the naked soul, the fulness of His grace to supply every want, and His ability in every respect to save to the uttermost all that come unto God by Him.

May that precious gospel, of which Christ crucified is the sum and substance, appear to me in all its truth, as the testimony of God, in all its sacred importance as the word of life; in all its fulness, its suitableness to my case, its preciousness, and its glory, that I may be enabled to receive it with full and entire approbation, as a system most honourable to God and safe for man, and that I may believe it with my whole heart.

Let me be a partaker of that faith which is connected with unfeigned repentance of sin, a sincere attachment to Jesus Christ, a subjection of heart and life to His will and government, an holy indifference to all that this present world can afford, and a sincere and constant endeavour to obey Thy commands. May I receive and embrace the truth as it is in Jesus, so that it may dwell and abide in me, in all its sacred energy and sanctifying power, working effectually in me, as it does in all them that believe. Thus let my heart be purified by faith, and give me an inheritance among them who are sanctified by faith which is in Thee. Nor let me be a stranger to the joy of faith; but fill me with all that joy and peace in believing, which arise from the view and manifestation of pardoning mercy, through the precious blood of Thy dear Son; to whom with Thyself, and the blessed Spirit, the one eternal God, be equal and endless praises. Amen.

Chapter Three

The Evidence Believers Give That Christ Is Precious To Them

God hath magnified His love, and set forth the riches of His grace towards us, in a manner which should effectually allure our hearts to Him. While we were enemies, and rebels in open arms against Him, He was pleased to send His beloved Son to die for our sins, in order to redeem us from death. He who is the brightness of His Father's glory, and the express image of His person, became a man of sorrows for our sakes. In the greatness of His condescension, He called Himself the Son of man, but all the fulness of the God-head dwelt bodily in Him. He was declared to be God manifest in the flesh. He came down from His Father's bosom, and became man, not to condemn the world of mankind. but to expose His life and blood for our sakes; to make His soul an offering for our sins, to sustain inconceivable anguish and sorrow, and to die for us, that He might bring us back to God and happiness. He poured out His soul to death, to secure us from the deserved wrath and vengeance of God. He was wounded for our transgressions, He was bruised for our iniquities. The chastisement of our peace was upon Him, that we through His stripes might be healed. He was stricken and smitten of God, and afflicted, that He might open the way for us to partake of Divine mercy, and render the offended Majesty of heaven a more proper, and a more engaging object of our love.

He is the beloved Son of God, the first and the everlasting favourite of heaven, the highest object of His Father's delight; He is the great peace-maker between God and sinners, the chief messenger of divine love to men. If He had not undertaken to make peace by the blood of His cross, we should have continued the children of wrath for ever. We should have been in the same state with the fallen angels, for whom no Saviour is provided, and to whom no promise of pardon and reconciliation is made. To us the Child was born, to *us* the Son was given. He came to deliver us from our state of enmity and rebellion, to save us from sin and its awful consequences; from the curse of God's righteous law, and from everlasting destruction. His heart was pierced for the sake of sinful men. The messages of His own, and of His Father's love, He has written to us in lines of blood; He sealed the covenant of peace between God and man with the blood of His cross, which He shed for us, to procure the remission of our sins. This is the divine Saviour who, though disregarded by many, is precious to those that believe. I now proceed, *To consider what evidence they give that He is precious to them.*

SECTION 1

IF CHRIST IS PRECIOUS TO US, WE SHALL TRUST OUR EVERLASTING CONCERNS IN HIS HANDS.

The apostle Peter, when he speaks of Christ being precious to them that believe, represents Him under the idea of a foundation. "Wherefore also it is contained in the Scripture, Behold I lay in

Zion a chief corner-stone, elect, precious: and he that believeth on Him shall not be confounded. Unto you therefore which believe He is precious;" that is, precious under that consideration particularly; and you shew it, by making it your chief design and care to be found built upon Him, as the sure foundation.

They who trust in their own hearts, and go about to establish their own righteousness like the unbelieving Jews, do, like them, stumble at the stumbling-stone. To such Christ cannot be said, in any sense, to be precious; since they set themselves directly to oppose the very design of His coming into this world, which was, that He might be "the end of the law for righteousness to every one that believeth." That man is no true believer in Jesus who rests in the law, and endeavours to lay a foundation of hope contrary to that which is laid, even Jesus Christ. He seeks not righteousness by faith, but as it were by the works of the law.

But he, to whom the Saviour of sinners is precious, is dead to the law by the body of Christ, that he may live unto God. He places all his confidence for acceptance with the Father, and for everlasting life, in that divine Redeemer in whom the Gentiles trust. He worships God in the spirit, he rejoices in Christ Jesus and has no confidence in the flesh. He knows whom he has believed, and is persuaded that that almighty Saviour is able to keep what he has committed unto Him until that day. In short, all his hopes centre in Him.

Hence the sacred writers so frequently speak of the actual out-goings of a gracious soul towards Jesus Christ, for salvation, of looking and coming to Him, of receiving Him, and of trusting in Him. This is something more than giving credit to the testimony which is given concerning Him; something different from the belief of the truth. But at the same time, he who really, and from his heart, believes what God's word reveals concerning the nature of sin, his own vile and lost condition, together with the glorious way in which sinners are saved by Jesus Christ, will necessarily be induced to flee to Him to receive Him, and to rest upon Him for the salvation of his soul. It must be so in the very nature of things. How could the enlightened sinner give evidence that Christ is precious to him, as one who is able to save to the uttermost, if he himself have no degree of hope, trust or confidence in Him, under that considerations. Hence, though this dependence on the Redeemer for salvation, is distinct from the belief of the truth concerning Him, it is distinct from it only as an inseparable effect is distinct from its cause. Faith and trust may be distinguished, but they cannot be divided. Some degree of hope or trust in Christ appears to be the necessary and immediate effect of believing what the gospel reveals concerning Him. When the sinner understands and realizes what God says of the evil of sin, of the misery of fallen man, and of the appointed way of salvation by a glorious and all-sufficient Mediator, he, in consequence, flies for refuge to the hope set before him, and ventures the whole weight of his everlasting interests in His hands.

The convinced sinner is deeply impressed with a sense of the insufficiency of his own works; he has given up all hope of acceptance with God by any thing which he hath done, or ever can do; if we therefore suppose him to have no trust in the Saviour of sinners, he must be in a state of absolute despair; and this is entirely inconsistent with that faith which, as we have seen, implies the choice and approbation of God's way of saving sinners by Jesus Christ. Hope and trust are the immediate and natural consequences of such believing views of the propriety and glory of the Divine remedy, as have been mentioned in the former chapter.

A great deal is said in the Old Testament concerning hope and trust. The term faith very rarely occurs. But the hope and trust so frequently spoken of by Moses, David and the prophets, certainly comprehend and include what is called faith, by the writers of the

New Testament. Hope and trust sweetly compose the soul of a regenerate man, and bring him into that state of rest and tranquility which is so desirable, amidst the fluctuations and disquietudes to which human life is subject. All the rest we enjoy in this world is connected with trust in God. "Thou wilt keep him in perfect peace whose mind is stayed on Thee; because he trusteth in Thee." The special object of this trust is God, reconciled unto us through the mediation of His Son. Respect must be had to this mediation, where the goodness, the mercy, the grace, the name, the faithfulness, or the power of God is mentioned, as that on which the soul relies. For none of these can be the object of a helpless sinner's trust, but on account of that covenant which is confirmed and ratified by the blood of the Redeemer. When the infinite mercy of God is spoken of in particular, as that in which we are to confide, we are to understand by it, His unbounded grace, setting forth Jesus Christ, as the propitiation for our sins. Trust in this mercy is what the apostle calls "receiving the atonement." Receiving it denotes our approbation of it, and our confiding in it, as the great effect of Divine wisdom, goodness, faithfulness, love and grace, which can never fail those who rely upon it.

It is not the part of wisdom, in natural things, to trust any one with affairs of importance before we know Him; if we should do so, though perhaps our concerns may be safe in His hands, yet every discouraging circumstance, every flying report, will be ready to shake our hearts, and fill us with fear. The Christian knows whom he has believed; or, as the word used by the apostle signifies, whom he has trusted. Athenians may build their altars to an unknown God; but Christians trust not in an unknown Redeemer. "They that know Thy name," O God our Saviour, "will put their trust in Thee."

This trust consists in a committing of the guilty helpless soul to the care of Christ, who is commissioned by His almighty Father to take care of lost souls, and to save them with an everlasting salvation. It is a secret application of the heart to Christ, in which we resign our guilty persons to Him, to be pardoned for the sake of His sufferings; our naked souls to be clothed in His righteousness; our sinful and polluted natures to be sanctified by the power of His grace, and to be made meet for everlasting glory.

We are encouraged thus to trust in Him under a full persuasion of His ability to save to the uttermost. We know that He is mighty to save. We are assured that His obedience unto death was perfect and complete; that His blood cleanseth from all sin; that His righteousness render those who believe accepted with the Father, unto eternal life; that His power and grace are sufficient to conquer all our disorderly passions, to support us under all our temptations, to purify our hearts, to strengthen our endeavours in the practice of holiness, and to keep us safely to His heavenly kingdom.

This trust differs from a feeble belief of the words, the works, and the power of Christ, upon hearsay, or slight notice; it is built upon just and certain evidence. The believer hath abundant testimony to the truth of Christ's being able to save. God Himself hath given witness from heaven, by miracles, visions, and voices. The apostles, prophets, and martyrs, have filled the earth with their witness; and by most convincing arguments, have proved the all-sufficiency of the Redeemer. The Christian has a witness in his own soul, to the power and grace of Christ, when he feels the sanctifying efficacy of the gospel upon his heart, and experiences Divine peace in his conscience, with the sweet foretastes of immortal felicity.[11] Christ is precious on account of all those glorious qualifications which render Him the fittest object of a sinner's hope and trust, and the believer gives evidence of this in his own case, by entrusting his everlasting concerns to His hands.

---

11   Dr. Watts

SECTION 2

IF CHRIST IS PRECIOUS UNTO US, WE SHALL DELIGHT TO
THINK OF HIM, TO HEAR OF HIM, AND TO SPEAK OF HIM.

The Christian knows that his future blessedness will consist in
being where Jesus is, and beholding His glory; and he concludes,
that frequent contemplation of Him in the present state, must have
a tendency, through Divine grace, to prepare him for that happy
state which he has in prospect. "For we all with open face, beholding, as in a glass, the glory of the Lord, are changed into the same
image from glory to glory, even as by the Spirit of the Lord."[12]

A learned, pious and aged divine makes use of the following
expressions, when speaking of the importance and utility and habitual contemplation on the glory and excellency of Christ: "If we
desire to have faith in its vigour, or love in its power, giving rest,
complacency, and satisfaction to our souls, we are to seek for them
in the diligent discharge of this duty; elsewhere they will not be
found. Herein would I live; herein would I die. Hereupon would
I dwell in my thoughts and affections, to the withering and con-
sumption of all the painted beauties of this world; to the crucify-
ing of things here below, till they become as worthless, dead, and
deformed, no way meet for affectionate embraces."

The believer will surely take pleasure in musing on the glories and excellencies of His adorable Redeemer. The object of our
warmest affection will be much in our thoughts. "My meditation
of Him," says the Psalmist, "shall be sweet. In the multitude of my

---

12   To know God, and to love Him, constitute a man holy upon earth; to know God,
     and to love Him, will constitute a man happy in heaven. God is the supreme *truth*;
     and all the intelligence, all the knowledge of our *minds* ought to relate to Him, as
     to their object. God is the supreme *good*, and all the motions of our *wills* ought
     to tend towards Him, as towards their only and last end. On this principle Jesus
     Christ has founded the religion and worship, which we profess.—'*Flechier*, Serm.
     Pour la Pentecote, tom.ii.

thoughts within me, Thy comforts delight my soul." It appears from the writings of this holy man, that he employed a considerable portion of his time, amidst all the business and the cares which came upon him as the governor of a numerous people, in meditating on the word, the statutes, and the testimonies of God; and he ever found something in them worthy of his high esteem, and his holy joy. "O how I love Thy law? It is my meditation all the day. I have seen an end of all perfection, but Thy commandments are exceeding broad." He was particularly delighted in contemplating the glories of the expected Messiah. "My heart," says he, "is inditing a good matter; I speak of the things which I have made, meditated and composed, concerning the King; my tongue is the pen of a ready writer. Thou art fairer than the children of men. Gird Thy sword upon Thy thigh, O most Mighty, with Thy glory and Thy majesty."[13]

"Shall not my thoughts," says the believer, "be frequently employed in meditating on the love of that infinitely glorious person,

---

13 A right knowledge of the Lord Jesus Christ will fill the mind with thoughts and meditations concerning Him so as to excite the affections to cleave to Him with delight. A discovery of the glory of His person, of the perfection of His atoning sacrifice, and of the fulness of His grace, must inspire the heart with love to Him; and it is the tendency of love to excite in the mind of many thoughts about the beloved object. He that lives the blessed life of faith in the Son of God, will frequently think of his Saviour; of what he is in Himself, of His love, of His condescension, and of the manifestation of all the glorious excellencies of the Divine nature in Him, for the recovery and salvation of men. It is much to be lamented, that those who profess a sincere attachment to the Redeemer should have their thoughts so little employed about Him. Where a multitude of worldly cares, desires, fears and hopes prevail in the mind, they cumber and perplex it, so as to bring on a great inaptitude to spiritual meditation. The advice of the apostle Paul is of great importance in this as in other cases: "If ye then be risen with Christ, seek those things which are above, where Christ sitteth at the right hand of God. Set your affection (your mind, your thoughts,) on things above, not on things on the earth. For (with respect to this present world, according to what you profess) ye are dead, and your life is hid with Christ in God." Earthly and sensual affection fill the hearts and heads of men with multitudes of thoughts concerning those objects on which they are fixed, so as to leave no room, nor indeed inclination for spiritual and heavenly thoughts.

to whom I am indebted for deliverance from the greatest misery, and for all the hope I have of being one day advanced to everlasting glory and felicity!" He poured out His holy soul in agonies, under the curse of the avenging law, to make me a partaker of eternal blessedness. He perfectly fulfilled the precepts of that law, that I, by His obedience, might be made righteous.

> —*For me He liv'd.*
> *Toil'd for my ease, and for my safety bled.*
> *What heart of stone but glows at thoughts like these?*
> *Such contemplations mount us, and should mount*
> *The mind still higher; nor ever glance on man*
> *Unraptur'd, uninflam'd.*

The grand blessing which our Lord solicits and demands for His disciples, in His last solemn intercession is, that they may behold His glory. It is that which will complete the blessedness of heaven, and fill its inhabitants with joy unspeakable and full of glory. Surely, then, it should be our delight to anticipate, in some degree, that celestial bliss, and to habituate our souls to this sacred exercise, which will be our business and our reward for ever.

This glorious, this adorable Redeemer thought upon us long before the foundations of the world were laid. He bore us on His heart when He hung on the cross; when He was rent with wounds, and racked with pain; when He poured out His dying groans, and spilt His blood. He remembers us now, when He is exalted at the right hand of the Majesty in the heavens, and will never, never forget us, through all the ages of eternity. Surely, then, we ought to think of Him. Impressed with a sense of His everlasting kindness, we should be ready to say, as the captives in Babylon, concerning their beloved city Jerusalem, "If I forget Thee (O blessed Jesus) let my right hand forget her cunning; if I do not remember Thee, let my tongue cleave to the roof of my mouth."

—Remember thee!
Ah, my dear Lord, while memory holds a seat
In this devoted breast—Remember thee!
Yes from the table of my memory
I'll wipe away all trivial fond records,
Which youth and observation copy'd there,
And Thy remembrance all along shall live
Within the book and volume of my brain.

What holy transports of soul, what divine delights have many Christians experiences, in meditating on the glories of the Redeemer! Ascending the mount of contemplation their souls have taken wing, and explored the height and depth, the length and breadth of the love of Christ, which passeth knowledge. They have seen by the eye of faith, that He is infinitely amiable in Himself, that He is the admiration of angels, the darling of heaven, and the delight of the Father. They have viewed Him in the brightness of His ineffable glory, clothed with majesty and honour, which cannot be described. They have been transported with the smiles of His countenance, and said of Him, "He is the chiefest among ten thousand, and altogether lovely." They have then considered their own unworthiness, and said, "Can such a wretch as I be the object of His love? So vile a worm, so unprofitable a creature, so great a sinner, one so deserving of His everlasting abhorrence! Has He loved me, so as to give Himself for me? O what marvelous kindness is this. Is my worthless name written in His book of life? Am I redeemed by His blood, renewed by His Spirit, beautified with His comeliness, and clothed in His righteousness? O wonder of wonders; mystery beyond all mysteries! How can I forbear to love this adorable Saviour? Can I withhold my choicest affections from Him? Ah no! Had I a thousand lives, a thousand souls, they should all be devoted to Him. Ye tempting vanities of this lower world, ye flattering honours, ye deceitful riches, adieu! Jesus is my all: my light, my life, my unfailing treasure, my everlasting portion. Nothing below the skies is deserving of my love. Precious Redeemer in Thee the boundless wishes of my soul are filled, and all my inward powers rejoice in Thee. I long to quit this tenement of clay, and to rest in the bosom of Thy love for ever!"

That one who loves Jesus delights to hear of Him, and to converse about Him, cannot be doubted, since every man is best pleased with that intelligence, and that conversation in which the object of his dearest affections is the principal theme. It is on this account that the gospel is a joyful sound to him that believes, because it sets forth Christ in His glory. No sermons are so precious and so animating to him, as those in which the Redeemer's excellencies are most fully displayed. It is then that the Christian says, "I sit under His shadow with great delight, and His fruit is sweet unto my taste." A sermon which, as one of the ancients speaks, is not enlivened with the mellifluous name of Jesus, in which there is nothing of His atonement for sin, of His matchless love, and saving power, is heard with coolness and indifference; while the doctrine of the cross is as life from the dead.

SECTION 3

IF CHRIST BE PRECIOUS TO US, WE SHALL BE GRATEFUL FOR THE BENEFITS WE RECEIVE FROM HIM.

It must be acknowledged, that, like many who are more forward to borrow than to pay again, we are frequently more ready to ask favours at the hand of God, than to return thanks for those we receive from Him. An unhumbled heart sets not a due value on Divine mercies; but those who are truly acquainted with themselves, who know what they are and have been, together with what the Lord has done for them, in raising them up from the depths of sin and woe, will call upon their souls and all that is within them, to bless the holy name of their gracious Deliverer.

They will perhaps express their gratitude in some such language as the following:

"O Lord, I will praise Thee, for though Thou wast angry with me, Thine anger is turned away, and Thou comfortest me. Behold, God is my salvation, I will trust, and not be afraid; for the Lord Jehovah is my strength and my song; He also is become my salvation." "Eternally blessed be the propitious Redeemer, who, from the plentitude of heavenly bliss, and the highest exaltation of glory, descended to low mortality, and became obedient to death, even the death of the cross, to ransom my perishing soul, to rescue me from death and damnation, and to give me a lot among the righteous. How can I pretend to have a regard for Him, if I am not thankful for His benefits?

"Lord Thou hast raised me up out of an horrible pit, out of the miry clay: Thou hast set my feet upon a rock, and established my goings. Thou hast, I trust, graciously pardoned those hateful crimes which might have caused me eternal regret, and plunged me in everlasting misery. Thou hast given that tranquillity to my once troubled conscience, which is the anticipation of Paradise. Thou hast given me some hope of seeing Thy face here after with unutterable joy, and of dwelling at Thy right hand, where there are pleasures for evermore.

"Blessed be the Lord, who daily loadeth me with His benefits, while I am in the way to the promised inheritance. Thine, O Lord, is the air I breathe, the food I eat, and the raiment I put on. The intellectual powers of which I am possessed, the use of my reason, and a capacity of knowing, of loving, of serving, and of enjoying Thee, are among the best and choicest of Thy mercies. All the happiness, and, indeed, all the usefulness of my life, either to myself or others, are from Thee.

"Long ago might I have been cast off, as an unprofitable servant, who knew his Master's will, yet did it not. But Thy mercy is greater than the heavens, and the instances thereof are more in number than the sands upon the sea-shore. They are renewed every morning, and multiplied every moment.

"While I attempt to celebrate Thy praise, may I live to the glory of my ever bountiful Benefactor. It would be the excess of ingratitude to employ the favours I receive from Thee, in the violation of Thy commands. Every blessing of Thy hand furnishes me with a motive to serve Thee. Lord, I would shew forth Thy praise, not only with my lips, but in my life, by giving up myself to Thy service, and walking before Thee in holiness and righteousness all my days."

The religion we profess is far from requiring us perpetually to put on a mournful countenance. On the other hand it enjoins upon us cheerfulness, gratitude of heart, and joy in the Lord. It is an apostolic injunction, "Rejoice in the Lord alway, and again I say, rejoice." As if it had been said, "Endeavour to maintain an habitual joy, in Christ Jesus, and in the hopes and privileges you derive from Him; for the honour of your Divine Master, and the prosperity of your own souls are intimately connected with it. There is enough in the object of your affections to furnish you with matter of joy, even in the worst circumstances which can attend you in this world. The worldly man rejoices in his possessions, the voluptuous man in his vain pleasures, but ye are to rejoice in the Lord. Delight yourselves in Him, and He will give you the desire of your hearts. Serve Him with gladness, and come before His presence with singing."

When the Ethiopian eunuch became acquainted with Christ and His salvation, how was his heart cheered with the discovery! A new sun seemed to arise, and a new world to display its beauties around him. Every object brightened before him, and he "went on his way rejoicing." Christians, go ye and do likewise. Call upon your souls to magnify the Lord, and let your spirits rejoice in God your Saviour. His love, His goodness, His matchless and multiplied benefits demand this at your hands. If we derive not the same consolation from Christ and the gospel, which good men have formerly experienced, it must be owing to the weakness of our faith, and the want of sincerity, ardour and diligence in the service of God.

We are expressly commanded, "in every thing to give thanks." Whatever may be our present circumstances, our dependence on God, and our obligations to Him, require us to be habitually grateful to our Divine Benefactor, since we never can be attended with such afflictions as not to have greater cause for thankfulness than for complaint. We should reflect on our unworthiness of the least of all God's mercies, and on the riches of His undeserved grace, in loading us with benefits, which far over-balance all our afflictions. We should labour to keep up a cheerful, thankful frame of heart in every condition of life, for "the joy of the Lord is our strength."

It is the will of God in Christ Jesus, that we should in every thing, give thanks. By the gift of His Son for us, and the bestowment of His saving blessings on us, He has laid a foundation for perpetual thankfulness, which is every way sufficient to justify the reasonableness of the demand.

As it is my earnest wish that this little book may be of service to enkindle and promote devout affections in those who may peruse it, I hope the following lines, for part of which I am obliged to the seraphic Dr. Young, will not be thought unsuitable for the purpose:

> *To man the bleeding cross has promis'd all;*
> *The bleeding cross has sworn eternal grace;*
> *Who gave His life, what grace shall he deny?*
> *What cordial joy, what consolation strong!*
> *Whatever winds arise, or billows roll,*
> *Our int'rest's in the Master of the storm.*
> *Cling there, and in wreck'd nature's ruins smile*

Religion! thou the soul of happiness;
And, groaning Calvary, of thee!—There shine
The noblest truths; there strongest motives sting;
There, sacred violence assaults the soul;
There, nothing but compulsion is forborne.

O Thou my Sacrifice! My God! my all!
My theme! my inspiration! And my crown!
My strength in age! My rise in low estate!
My light in darkness! And my life in death!
My hope in time! bliss through eternity!
Eternity's too short to speak Thy praise,
Or fathom thy unbounded love to man,
To man of men the meanest, e'en to me'
'Tis this makes sacred triumph a command:
'Tis this makes joy a duty to the wise:
'Tis impious in a Christian to be sad.

Bound, er'ry heart: and ev'ry bosom burn!
O what a scale of miracles is here!
Its lowest round high-planted on the skies:
Its tow'ring summit lost beyond the thought
Of man or angel! O that I could climb
The wonderful ascent with equal praise!
Praise! flow for ever (if astonishment
Will give thee leave) my praise! for ever flow;
Praise ardent, cordial, constant, to high heaven,
More fragrant than Arabia sacrifie'd
And all her spicy mountains in a flame
O may I breathe no longer than I breathe
My soul in praise to Him, who gave my soul,
And all her infinite of prospect fair!

SECTION 4

IF CHRIST BE PRECIOUS TO US, WE SHALL PREFER HIM TO EVERY OTHER OBJECT: HE WILL HAVE THE CHIEF PLACE IN OUR AFFECTIONS.

The love which a Christian has to his Saviour, as a good writer observes, penetrates and possesses his heart. This distinguishes it from the feigned love of hypocrites, which is only in word, or in some external actions, while their hearts are full of sinful self-love, so that it may be said of them as God once said of the Israelites, "This people honour Me with their lips, but their hearts are far from Me."[14]

Divine love so possesses the heart, as not to allow a partition of it to inferior objects. Thus it is distinguished from that partial love which is sometimes found in unregenerate persons, which is only transient, and never comes to perfection; because the heart is divided, and occupied with various worldly objects. The love of Christ is not rooted, nor predominant in the mind.

A believer may, and, indeed, ought to love his fellow-creatures. A father should love his children, a husband his wife, and a friend his friend; but the character of love to Jesus is, on the one hand, to suffer no love contrary to itself to have place in the heart; for "no man can serve two masters, and the friendship of this world is enmity against God;" and, on the other hand, this divine affection does not suffer any of the objects, the love of which is in some degree compatible with itself, to hold the chief place in the heart. This chief place is for the Lord, whom we ought to love

---

14 Those religious performances which leave in our hearts the love of the world and its criminal pleasures, are rather a semblance of piety than piety itself. We are only before God what we are in heart and affection. He will be the object of all our desires, the end of all our actions, the principle of all our affections, the governing power of our whole souls. All that does not flow from these dispositions, all that does not either conduct us to these, or establish us in them, however shining before men, is nothing but a sounding brass and a tinkling cymbal.—*Masillon*, Tom. ii. *Careme.*

with supreme ardour. To regard Him only in a secondary way, is to provoke His resentment. The choicest affections of our souls ought to be supremely fixed upon Him.[15]

If this indeed be the case with us, we shall be induced to devote our souls and our bodies, our talents, our powers and our faculties, as a living sacrifice to Him. To contemplate His adorable perfections will be our highest joy. We shall be ready to obey Him in opposition to all the threats and the solicitations of men. We shall rely upon Him though all outward appearances seem to be against us, and rejoice in Him though we have nothing else to comfort us. If we enjoy health and plenty, friends and reputation, the Lord is still the object of our earnest desires and our supreme delight. "Whom have I in heaven but Thee, and there is none upon earth that I desire besides Thee. As the hart panteth for the water-brooks, so longeth my soul after Thee, O God. My soul thirsteth for God, for the living God; when shall I come and appear before God?"

The religion of Jesus does not consist in dull and lifeless formality. "God is a spirit, and they that worship Him must do it in spirit and in truth." Our hearts should be warmly and vigorously engaged in cleaving to Him; we should be fervent in spirit in serving the Lord. Such is the infinite excellency of Jesus Christ, the Author of eternal salvation, that there can be no suitableness in the exercises of our minds towards Him, unless they be lively and powerful. Lukewarmness is no where so odious and detestable as

---

15 That love which hath but created beings for its object, is degrading to the soul. It is a cleaving to that which can neither contribute to the happiness nor to the perfection of our nature; and, of course, which cannot give repose to our minds. For to love any object ardently, is to seek our felicity in it, and to expect that it will answer our wishes. It is to call upon it to fill that frightful void which we feel in ourselves, and to imagine that it is capable of giving us the satisfaction we seek. It is to regard it as the resource of all our wants, the remedy of all the evils which oppress us, and the source of all our happiness. Now, as it is God alone in whom we can find all these advantages, it is a debasing of the soul, it is idolatry to seek them in created objects.—*Masillon, ser pour la Careme, Tom. iv.*

here. There is something very significant in the apostles of Christ being said to be baptized with the Holy Ghost, and with fire, as it is expressive, among other things, of the fervour of those affections which the Spirit of God excited in their hearts.

The apostle Paul speaks of love, as of the greatest importance in religion. He represents it as the fountain whence proceeds all that is truly good. He speaks of it as that without which the greatest knowledge and gifts, and the most splendid profession, are vain and unprofitable. The sum of vital religion consists in this divine affection, and in those things which are the fruits of it. The children of God are described as those "that love the Lord Jesus Christ in sincerity."

This amiable apostle, in whom the true spirit of Christianity was so fully exemplified, gave every kind of evidence that Jesus Christ was precious to him. It appears from all his writings that this servant of the Lord was, in the whole course of his life, after his conversion, inflamed, actuated, and, as it were, swallowed up, by a most ardent love to his Divine Master. Hence he esteemed all things but loss for the excellency of the knowledge of Him, and counted them but dung that he might win Christ, and be found in Him. He declares that he was overpowered by this divine affection, and carried forward by it in the service of Him whom he so ardently loved, through all difficulties and sufferings. "For the love of Christ constraineth us;" not only His love to us, but our love to Him.

The knowledge a believer has of the excellency of Christ tends to raise in his mind a high esteem of Him. As it is impossible for any man to love an unknown object, so it cannot be expected that Christ should be supremely precious unto us, unless we know Him to be excellent and desirable, beyond whatever may be compared with Him. We shall not esteem Him above all things, if we have not elevated views of His transcendent worth.

We may possibly delight in some objects of an inferior nature, as they contribute to our health, our ease or our comfort. Our habitations, our food, and our other temporal enjoyments are dear to us, because they minister to our support and convenience in the present life. We have a compassionate regard for the poor, though perhaps we see little real excellency in their character. We feel our bowels of pity moved towards them, as fellow-creatures in distress. We have a natural attachment to our country and our kindred, because of their relation to us. But we love the Divine Saviour with a very superior kind of love. We know that He is in Himself possessed of the highest excellencies, and that He is able to bestow upon us the richest benefits. Our esteem of Him rises in proportion to the knowledge we have of Him. Good men therefore ardently desire to increase in the knowledge of Him, that their affections may be more intensely fixed upon Him.

And though the believer's regard for his Saviour is far from being wholly a selfish principle, yet the hope of interest in his favour serves to draw forth and confirm his attachment to Him. It seems impossible for any man to contemplate His supreme excellencies with delight, if he is destitute of hope. Christ is precious to those that believe, not to those who despair. The evil spirits said to Him, when He sojourned on earth, "We know Thee who Thou art, the Holy one of God;" but they know that there is no hope of their ever enjoying His favour; and therefore they continue in their enmity and rebellion against Him. Terror, slavish fear, and despair are so opposite to love, that the apostle John does not scruple to say concerning the Supreme Being, that it is a sense of His love to us which draws forth our attachment to Him; "We love Him because He first loved us." Much has been said, and perhaps with propriety, concerning love to Jesus Christ for His own infinite excellency, as being the most distinguishing proof of a real gracious affection; but at the same time, it does not appear either from the word of God, or from matter of fact, that this ever subsists in any mind destitute of hope. So far as slavish fear prevails, it is a bar to love; and therefore "he who fears" that Christ is not his friend, but may disown him at last, "is not made perfect in love." Hope of interest opens the springs of affection; it draws and attracts the hearts to its object. And therefore when we are required to give to our Maker and Sovereign our whole heart and mind, and soul and strength, the manner in which the command is expressed is worthy of peculiar notice, "Thou shalt love the Lord thy God."[16]

---

16   It is a maxim laid down by some respectable writers, that a *disinterested* love to God is *essential* to Christianity, or, as they express it, "Whoever seeks any thing in God beside God Himself, does not sincerely love Him." It is allowed, that God is in Himself an object infinitely amiable, that, were it possible for an intelligent being to exist independent on God, it would be impossible for such a being to contemplate the Divine Nature and not to love it. But it should be remembered, that, even in the case supposed, consciousness of conformity to the nature and fitness of things, would be attended with pleasure; and *pleasure* is *interest*; so that, strictly speaking, pure disinterested love to God seems to be impossible.

Good men love God under the severest strokes of His providence; but they find a pleasure in loving Him, and in submitting to His sovereign will, which amply indentifies them, and gives them the highest *interest* in this love. There are, as it should seem, not three different kinds of love to God, but three distinct *degrees* of the same love to Him. Our love may be drawn forth towards Him by the temporal benefits which we receive from His indulgent hand. Yet temporal blessings are not the objects of our supreme love; but God, the giver of them. Our love may be kindled and excited towards Him, by the spiritual blessings which He bestows upon us, according to the riches of His grace; such as His regarding and answering our prayers, His granting unto us discoveries of His mercy, in forgiving our sins, and the like, "I love the Lord," says the Psalmist, "because be hath heard the voice of my supplication." And then, God is to be loved for His own infinite amiableness and excellency. But this love, being attended with pleasure, cannot be separated from mental interest. "I love Him," says the most spiritual and heavenly-minded man upon earth, "who is the *health of my countenance, and my God. I will go to the altar of God; to God my exceeding joy.*" With respect to these three degrees of love, if the experience of Christians in common be attended to, it will perhaps be found, that most begin with the first, grow into the second, and end in the lest. And to the last, as to that degree which is most discriminating, most honourable, to God, and productive of the most noble effects, all good men should aspire. The question is not, whether men ought to love God disinterestedly; but, whether, in the fullest sense, it be possible to do so. "A Christian's desire." Says one of our old divines, "is to God *chiefly*, and to God *simply*; to God as the God of grace, for more strength and ability to serve Him; and to God as the God of all comfort, for the pleasure of fellowship and communion with Him."—*Dr. Horton's* Expos. of Psal. xlii.1'

If Jesus Christ is precious to us, the bent of our souls will be towards Him. We shall choose Him above and beyond every other object, as our most desirable portion, and exceeding great reward. If any thing in this world be chosen by us, as our chief good, our hearts will run out in strongest affections towards it. We shall look for our felicity in that object, be it what it may; that object therefore, and not Christ, will be most precious unto us.

If our regard for the Redeemer be supreme, as it ought to be, our whole hearts will go out after Him in the most intense longings, and with the most pleasing sensations. The heart of a believer is restless till it find its Saviour; till it obtain a solid hope and persuasion of His love, a growing conformity to Him, and sincere delight in Him. The soul rests and acquiesces in Him alone, and is not easy without the enjoyment of some tokens of His love. The language of such a one is, "If I have Christ for my friend, and my everlasting portion, I have all. When His face is hid, and His comforts withdrawn, I seek Him with restless desire, and often cry, O that *I knew where I might find Him!* After a season of darkness, when the light of His countenance is again lifted up upon me, I say, *Return unto thy rest, O my soul, for the Lord hath dealt bountifully with thee.*" [17]

The sense we have of our continual and absolute need of Christ has a tendency to engage our affections to Him. At our first conversion, when we were turned from darkness to light, we saw ourselves lost, and that none but Christ could save us; we felt the wounds of a guilty conscience, and we knew that He only could heal them; we trembled before the offended Majesty of heaven, and we were persuaded that He only could deliver us from the wrath to come. We saw that there was no remission of sin, no

---

17   For several hints in this part of the work. I am indebted to Dr. Watts, in his excellent *Discourse on the Love of God.*

reconciliation with God, no salvation but through Christ Jesus; hence He became, at that period, *all in all* to us.[18]

We still see the absolute necessity of this precious Saviour in every respect, so that without Him we can do nothing, as He Himself hath told us. We have need of Him, when we are dark, to enlighten us; when we are dull and lifeless, to quicken us; when we are straitened, to enlarge us; when we are weak, to strengthen us; when we are tempted, to succour us; when we have fallen, to raise and restore us; when we are full of doubts and perplexity, to satisfy us and give us peace; when we are disquieted with fears, to encourage us; when we are staggering at the promise of God through unbelief, to confirm our faith. As none but Christ can do these things for us, He must be precious to our souls.

The following aspiration shall close the present section:

"Reign, blessed Jesus, in my heart, reign supreme, and without a rival. Fain would I love Thee above all things in heaven or earth. I see that Thou art infinitely glorious in Thy ownself, and worthy of the highest esteem and love. Thou art the only all-sufficient good, the overflowing spring of grace and blessedness. All things beneath and besides Thee are vanity and emptiness. In comparison with

---

18   "God is love," saith the apostle *John*. The person of Christ, as clothed with human nature, is the first and full object of the love of the Father, in those acts of it which are towards any thing without Himself. In the prospect of His future incarnation and work, the Father says of Him, "Behold my servant whom I uphold mine elect in whom my soul delighteth." Christ is the first object of all that divine love which extends itself to man. It is all fixed upon Him, and by and through Him it is communicated unto the church. The prayer of our great Mediator runs in these words, "That the love wherewith Thou hast loved Me, may be in them." That is, "Incline their hearts to love Me, even as Thou hast loved Me." Hence our love to Christ is that in which our conformity to the image of God principally consists. In nothing do the children of God bear a greater likeness to Him, than in their love to Jesus Christ, who is the chief object of His love, in whom His soul doth rest with everlasting satisfaction and delight. Where love to the Divine Redeemer is wanting in my mind, there is nothing of the image of God. And therefore, says the apostle Paul, "If any man love not our Lord Jesus Christ, let him be *anathema maranatha;*" he bears no likeness to God; his mind is wholly carnal; and, as such, he lies under a dreadful curse, till the Lord shall come, if his heart be not changed.

Thee, they are less than nothing. Hast not Thou drawn my heart towards Thyself, and made me willing to make choice of Thee, as my Saviour, and my Portion? I would renounce all that the world calls good or great, that I may be entirely Thine. Be Thou my everlasting inheritance, and I shall want nothing that a whole world of creatures can bestow. Whom have I in heaven but Thee, and what is there on earth that I desire in comparison of Thee.

"I am but a stranger in this world, wherever I may be situated, or however I may happen to be distinguished. And surely it is my privilege that I am so. When I look not upon myself as a stranger and a pilgrim, when I am captivated with any thing in this place of my exile, I forget myself, and act far beneath my character, as a candidate for an immortal crown.

"I hope I have counted the cost of being one of Thy disciples; I hope I have laid in the balance all that with which this world can flatter me, and compared it with the gain of godliness. The odds I find to be infinite. I would therefore bid adieu to the gaudy pomps and empty vanities of life and give my heart to heaven. I hear the voice of infinite mercy directing me to set my affections on things above. I would obey the celestial Monitor. What can present scenes afford, to tempt me to relinquish the choice I have been enabled to make? What can they offer, as an equivalent to His favour, whose smiles enlighten the realms of bliss, and fill all the inhabitants of heaven with unbounded and ever lasting delight?

SECTION 5

IF CHRIST IS PRECIOUS TO US, WE SHALL SINCERELY DESIRE HIS PRESENCE, AND LONG TO ENJOY INTIMATE COMMUNION WITH HIM.

It is well known that this is the tendency of a sincere attachment, whoever be the object of it. Hence we desire to have the company of our dear friends and relations. Absence is one of the sharpest pains of love. Our blessed Redeemer has said, "He that loveth Me shall be loved of My Father, and I will love him, and will manifest Myself to him." If He be precious unto us, we shall earnestly desire the fulfilment of that promise, that He would make known unto us more and more of the loveliness of His person, and of His special kindness and love to our souls. Distance from Him, the suspension of His favour, or the hidings of His face, will give us pain. We shall often say, "Lord, when wilt Thou come unto me, according to Thy promise? Let me find Thee graciously near, assuring my soul that I am Thine, and that Thou art mine for ever. Fill my heart with those heavenly comforts and holy joys which Thou bestowest on them that love Thee. I cannot bear this absence from Thee. Come, Lord Jesus, dwell in my heart by faith, that I being rooted and grounded in love, may be able to comprehend with all saints, what is the breadth and length, the depth and heighth; and to know Thy love which passeth knowledge; that I may be filled with all the fulness of God.[19]

---

19   When the eyes of men are opened to see their sin, their danger by it, and the insufficiency of their own works to justify and save them, no object is so desirable to them as the Lord Jesus Christ. The riches, the honours, and the pleasures of the world are but vanity and emptiness to them in comparison with Him. He is therefore said to be the "desire of all nation," because men in all nations under heaven, who are made sensible of their need of Him uniformly desire acquaintance with Him, and an interest in Him above every thing else. Their desires, like so many needles touched by the loadstone, have all a tendency to Him as their centre. They all meet in Him as the same blessed object.

Were those who are illuminated by His Spirit and grace collected together from the remotest corners of the earth, it would be found, on the strictest examination, that their desires have all the same tendency. Now, that which is the object of our ardent desire is precious in our estimation. To win our hearts the divine Redeemer died. To draw men unto Himself was the end He had in view when He became obedient unto death, even the death of the cross. "And I, if I be lifted up from the earth, will draw all men unto Me." Surely such a Saviour is worthy of our warmest desires, and our most fervent love. While others are in such a state of blindness and infatuation, as to see no beauty or excellency in Him that they should desire Him, to those who believe he is so precious that the desire of their souls is to His name, and to the remembrance of Him. But as bread and water are made necessary and desirable by hunger and thirst, so this desire after Christ, springs from a sense of need.

"Come down from on high, Thou Sovereign of my heart; take possession of me for Thyself. Inspire me with that holy flame of spiritual affection, that my soul may offer up the perpetual incense of holy love and desire towards Thee.

"O may all the alluring trifles and vain delights of this world stand aloof from my heart; for I have devoted it to my Redeemer for a habitation. Keep your distance, ye captivating delusions, from the gates of that temple where He only should dwell. There may He reign alone, over all my powers for ever.

"I seek after Him in His public ordinances; I search for Him daily in my retired devotions; I there give my soul a greater latitude, where no eye beholds me, where no ear can hearken to my vows. There I tell Him all my heart, in secret groans and cries. He knows what my sighs mean, and what are my fears, and my painful sorrows. There I blush before Him for my secret sins, and pour out the tear of penitential sorrow. There I utter my bitter complaints, of the disorderly passions I daily feel within me; I lament over the vanity of my thoughts, and spread before His eyes all my sores and diseases. I lay myself low in the dust at His feet, and tell Him with humble confusion of face how much I have done to dishonour Him, how unworthy I am of His notice, and yet how I long for communion with Him.

"O when shall these days of sin and temptation, these tedious seasons of absence and distance from my God and Saviour, have and end? I breathe out from time to time, the most earnest desires after Him, and after the endearing sensations of His love. My soul thirsteth for God, the living God; when shall I come and appear before God?"

> *My passions fly to seek their King,*
> *And send their groans abroad;*
> *They beat the air with heavy wing,*
> *And mourn an absent God.*

Round the creation wild I rove,
And search the globe in vain;
There's nothing here that's worth my love
Till He return again.

Pensive I climb the sacred hills,
And near Him vent my woes;
Yet His sweet face He still conceals,
And still my passion grows.

How long shall my poor panting soul
Seek Thee, my Lord, in vain?
Reveal Thy love, my fears control,
And ease me of my pain.

Thy presence, gracious Lord, can cheer
This dungeon where I dwell;
'Tis paradise when Thou art here;
When Thou art gone, 'tis hell.

Immortal joys Thy smiles impart;
Heav'n dawns in every ray;
One glimpse of Thee will ease my heart,
and turn my night to day.

SECTION 6

IF CHRIST IS PRECIOUS TO US, WE SHALL BE CONCERNED THAT OTHERS MAY KNOW AND LOVE HIM.

It is the nature of love wish well to the beloved object, and, if possible, to do good to Him who has a place in our hearts. Now, since the blessed Redeemer can receive no good from us, all we can do is, to be heartily concerned for the manifestation of His excellencies and honours among men. And this concern we shall surely feel if our hearts are right in His sight.

The apostle Paul, in whom every part of the Christian character was exemplified to a right degree, expressed a most earnest solicitude for the conversion and salvation of the Jesus. On this subject we find him declaring the sentiments and feelings of his heart in the following awful and pathetic manner: "I say the truth in Christ, I lie not, my conscience also bearing me witness in the Holy Ghost. That I have great heaviness, and continual sorrow in my heart: for I could wish that myself were accursed from Christ, (or after the example of Christ) for my brethren, my kinsmen according to the flesh." The sense of these last words appear to be this, "As Christ subjected Himself to the course, that He might deliver us from it, I think I could be content to be made an *anathema* after His example, and be like Him exposed to all the execrations of an enraged people, and even to the infamous and accursed death of crucifixion, if my brethren and kinsmen according to the flesh might hereby be delivered from their blindness, unbelief and impenitence, and be partakers of the blessings of the Redeemer's kingdom." This is true Christian heroism in its highest purity and excellence. While we talk of our regard for the Redeemer, what sentiments of compassion do we feel for those who are strangers to Him? Are we willing to submit to the most pressing difficulties, and do we think nothing too great to be done, too great to be borne, if their conversion and salvation might thereby be promoted?

Among the heathens we find whole nations, who trained up their children in a regard for the public good, as the highest object and the noblest end of all their cares. We meet with heroes among them, who eternized their names by their zeal for the welfare of their fellow-citizens. We find a Phocion, who, in taking that poison which was presented to him by his cruel persecutors, exhorted his son to cherish them, because he still owed more to his country than to his father: and Aristides, who, in going out to a banishment to which he was unjustly condemned, lifted up his eyes to heaven, and prayed, that the Athenians might never have cause to remember the cruelties they had exercised on his person: a Codrus, who, having learnt that the oracle had promised victory to the people whose prince should perish in war, devoted himself to death. It would be easy to extend the list, by mentioning Camillus, Sertorius, Paulus Æmilius, and others, famous in the page of ancient history, for this virtue. But the apostle of the Gentiles excelled them all, as far as the gospel he preached surpasses the dictates of the heathen moralists.

"Brethren," says he, to the converts at Rome, "My heart's desire and prayer to God for Israel is, that they might be saved." They were in a state of impenitence and unbelief; they made light of Christ, and persecuted His followers, having a zeal for God, but not according to knowledge. The apostle longed after them all in the bowels of Jesus Christ. The steady belief of God's secret purposes was no check upon his ardour for their conversion. He sought it of Him who only could effect it, sought it with the greatest earnestness and constancy. He knew their destruction was inevitable, if they continued in unbelief and impenitence. The salvation of souls appeared to him in all its magnitude, as that which had employed the counsels of Jehovah from eternity; that which the Son of God spent His life and shed His blood to procure; and that which is of infinite moment to sinners themselves. Hence arose the ardour of His mind in this noble cause.

He to whom Jesus is precious, who has himself experienced the power and sweetness of His saving love, will be ready to say to others, with the Psalmist, "O taste and see that the Lord is good; blessed are all they that trust in Him." Such a one will use his endeavours to bring his fellow-sinners under the means; he will discover his love to them and compassion for them by seasonable hints, exhortation and entreaties; he will earnestly pray that the word which they hear may savingly profit them; he will be careful to lay no stumbling-block before them; he will try to convince them of their danger, and to inform them where their help lies; he will strive to recommend the good cause, and to win their souls to make choice of it, by the meekness of wisdom, the labour of love, and the attractive power of a humble and holy conversation.

SECTION 7

IF CHRIST IS PRECIOUS TO US, WE SHALL BE GRIEVED WHEN HE IS DISHONOURED.

The sins of those who pretended some regard for the gospel, but lived not under the influence of its sanctifying truths, excited the sorrow of the apostle Paul, because the author of the gospel was precious to Him. "Of these," says he to the Philippians, "I have told you often, and now tell you, even weeping, that they are the enemies of the cross of Christ." He could not think of them, though they were enemies, without weeping, nor make mention of them in his letter, without bedewing the page with tears.

It is the burden of a Christian's heart, that the commands of Him who made the world, who gave being to all things, and who gave Himself for us that He might redeem us from all iniquity, should be trampled upon, and disregarded by men in general; and more especially, that this should be the case with any who profess to hope for salvation by Him.

A pious man cannot but be more particularly grieved for the sins of that city, town, congregation, or family to which he belongs, than for those of others. When Lot sojourned amongst the Sodomites, "that righteous man, dwelling among them, in seeing and hearing, vexed his righteous soul from day to day on account of their unlawful deeds." And the prophet Jeremiah most pathetically wished that his head were waters, and his eyes fountains of tears, that he might weep day and night, for the sins, and consequent calamities of his countrymen. In another place he thus addresses them, "But if ye will not hear, my soul shall weep in secret places for your pride, mine eye shall weep sore, and run down with tears."

A true Christian is a child of God; and it must grieve and distress him to see his heavenly Father so greatly offended and dishonoured as He is by many. He is a disciple of Jesus, and loves his Divine Master; hence he cannot but be distressed that men should make light of Him, of His gospel, His authority and commands. He is fully persuaded that they who sin against Him, wrong their own souls, and that all they that hate Him love death, or that which will issue in their own destruction.[20] Under such considerations as these the Psalmist broke out in the following strong

---

20   The stain of sin can only be washed away by blood; this intimates that sin deserves death. It is not the length of time employed in committing sin, which ought to decide as to the degree or the duration of its punishment; but the nature and the atrociousness of the offence.

Sin is a slighting every instance of God's goodness with which we are surrounded. The earth which sustains us, the sun which enlightens us, the food which nourishes us, and, in short, all the creatures designed to our use, are so many motives to obedience, and consequently are so many aggravations of our guilt and ingratitude, in rebelling against a good and gracious God. But let us consider the greatness of that Being against whom sin is committed. Approach to His throne; His eyes are as a flaming fire; the majesty of His glory fills heaven and earth. Regard the celestial hosts, who are the ministers of His will. And especially consider, that this great God is united to mortal flesh, to the end that He might suffer for us all that which the fury of men, all that which the rage of devils could imagine to be most rigorous; and then think what the nature of sin is, as committed against such a Being. To hate such a God, to despise such a Saviour, to trample on His laws, to disregard His gospel, and to be unawed by His threatenings, is deserving of the deepest hell. That burning lake, that eternal misery, with its unfathomable deeps, devils with their rage, hell with its horrors, have nothing in them which seems too severe for rebels capable of such astonishing ingratitude.

Charles the Ninth, king of France, sent a message to the Prince of Conde, a zealous protestant, and gave him three things to choose; to go to mass, or to be put to death, or to suffer banishment for life. The Prince nobly answered, "The first I will never choose, God helping me, for I abhor the idolatry of the mass; but for the two other, I leave it to the choice of the king, to do as he pleases. For there is more evil in the least sin, than in the greatest misery."

expressions: "Rivers of waters run down mine eyes, because men keep not Thy law."

I cannot forbear observing, that there are many causes for this grief at the present day; and if the Redeemer be indeed precious to us, our hearts must be affected while we are witnesses to the dishonour done to Him by multitudes about us. If we look into the professing world, we shall find many, who, on account of their scandalous lives, may justly be denominated the enemies of the cross of Christ. They profess to know Him, and to believe in Him, but in works they deny Him.

Many openly oppose the important doctrines of His proper deity; of His atonement for sin; of the work of His blessed Spirit on the hearts of men, in bringing them nigh to God; and of justification and salvation by His death. This cannot but give pain to those who, with the apostle Paul, are fully persuaded, that other foundation for the hope of sinners, no man can lay, than that which is laid, which is Jesus Christ; who believe, according to the Scriptures, that there is no other name under heaven, given among men, whereby we must be saved. It appears to them, that an opposition to these leading truths of the gospel, carries in it an attempt to rob the Redeemer of His glory, to take the crown from His head, and to overthrow that whole system of evangelical truth which is held forth in the New Testament: since the leading design of this system is, "That we might believe that Jesus is the Christ, the Son of God, and that believing, we might have life through His name."

There are others again, who profess to believe the truth, and yet show little or no regard to it, in a practical way. The power of godliness is, in many places, manifestly on the decline. Iniquity abounds, and the love of many is waxen cold. That charity which is the very bond of perfectness, is rarely to be found; few indeed there are who love one another with a pure heart fervently. Many seem to content themselves with mere speculations in religion, and that dead faith which the word of God condemns, is unprofitable. While in others, the cares of this world, the deceitfulness of riches, and the lusts of other things choke the word which they hear, so that it becometh unfruitful. Instead of having their conversation in heaven, they mind earthly things, and seem to be intent on gaining the world, though they lose their own souls in the vain pursuit. Others turn aside from the holy commandment which was delivered unto them, and fall into such scandalous practices as give great occasion to the enemies of the Lord to blaspheme.

He that loves the Lord Jesus Christ in sincerity, or, in other words, he to whom the divine Redeemer is precious, must be greatly distressed to think that he should be thus wounded in the house of his professed friends.

If we look into the world at large, we find every thing to shock and disquiet a serious mind. The whole world, saith the apostle John, lieth, is buried or entombed, in wickedness.

The abominable sin of drunkenness is practiced every where, by those whose god is their belly, and who glory in their own shame. The unclean spirit seems to have full possession of others, who live in the detestable, infatuating, and ruinous vice of lewdness, and are hurried on by their ungovernable passions, from bad to worse, from one degree of wickedness to another. The mouths of many are full of cursing and bitterness; their common discourse is interlarded with profaneness and blasphemy. The hearts of those who fear God are wounded, and their ears are stunned by multitudes, who, on all occasions, take His holy and sacred name in vain, and call for damnation on their own souls, and on the eyes, the bodies, and the souls of others. Our streets, our roads, and all our public places are crowded with diabolical monsters of this description, in the shape of men, who might seem to have studied the language of the bottomless pit. "Because of swearing the land mourneth."

The profanation of the Lord's day is grown to an amazing height. Nothing tends more to the increase of vice and wickedness. It is an inlet to sin of every kind. What sense of God and of duty is likely to be kept up, when divine worship is wholly neglected, and that day is entirely devoted to sensual gratification, and spent in the service of sin and Satan, which ought to be employed in acts of devotion and piety? The profanation of the Sabbath has, in many instances, been a leading step to an infamous end.

The man to whom Jesus is precious must be disquieted on account of these and many other abominations, which are constantly practised in the world. What proof do we give of regard to His law, His name, or His honour, if we are unmoved by these things? "I beheld transgressors, and was grieved, because they kept not Thy law." Dr. Doddridge's pathetic verses on these words of the pious Psalmist shall close this section.

> *Arise, my tend'rest thoughts, arise;*
> *To torrents melt my streaming eyes;*
> *And thou, my heart, with anguish feel*
> *Those evils which thou canst not heal.*
>
> *See human nature sunk in shame;*
> *See scandals pour'd on Jesus' name;*
> *The Father wounded through the Son;*
> *The world abus'd; the soul undone.*
>
> *See the short course of vain delight*
> *Closing in everlasting night;*
> *In flames which no abatement know,*
> *Though briny tears for ever flow.*
>
> *My God! I feel the mournful scene;*
> *My bowels yearn o'er dying men;*
> *And fain my pity would reclaim,*
> *And snatch the fire-brands from the flame.*

But feeble my compassion proves,
And can but weep where most it loves:
Thy own all-saving arm employ,
And turn these drops of grief to joy.

SECTION 8

IF CHRIST IS PRECIOUS TO US, WE SHALL BE
READY TO DENY OURSELVES FOR HIM.

If we judge of our regard for Jesus merely by the fervency and frequency of our emotions towards Him, we shall, at some seasons, perhaps, have painful suspicions respecting our sincerity. He Himself has been pleased to give us a safe and proper rule of judgment in this case: "If ye love Me, keep My commandments. He that hath My commandments and keepeth them, he it is that loveth Me." His word and will have a prevailing, governing influence on the hearts and lives of those to whom He is precious. A steady desire and endeavour to avoid those things which are displeasing in His sight, is a practical proof that He is dear to us.

To deny ourselves is, to give up our own supposed wisdom, that we may be entirely under the guidance of God, to resign our own wills that we may be subject to His will, and to yield our passions to His government. It is to forego every thing sinful to which self is inclined, to practice every good thing to which self is averse, and to be ready to give up every thing dear to ourselves at the call of God; as our ease, our friends, our goods, our health, or even our life. It is a disowning, or renouncing ourselves for Christ; making ourselves nothing that He may be all. This cannot be done unless He is precious to us, or, which is the same thing, unless He is the object of our supreme affection. But if this be the case, we shall give up ourselves, with all that we have, to Him, without making any reserve. We shall, on a deliberate counting of the cost, choose the religion of Jesus, with all that appertains to it; choose it as attended with all its difficulties. So Moses chose to suffer affliction with the people of God, rather than to enjoy the pleasures of sin which are but for a season, esteeming the reproach of Christ greater riches than the treasures of Egypt.

This is what our Lord means by the strong figurative expressions of plucking out the right eye, and cutting off the right hand; that is, parting with every thing dear to us, when it stands in competition with Him, or is opposed to His service or His honour. For He justly reminds us, that "no man can serve two masters; either he will hate the one, and love the other; or else he will hold to the one, and despise the other." He constantly teaches us the necessity of preferring Him and His interest and service to the dearest objects on earth. "For he that loveth father or mother, son or daughter more than Me, is not worthy of Me. And he that taketh not his cross, and followeth after Me, is not worthy of Me." When matters come to such a crisis, that a man must either break with his nearest and dearest relations and friends, or break with Christ, he that prefers their favour and friendship to Him, and will not give up temporal endearments for His sake, is not worthy to be owned as one of His real disciples, nor can he partake of the spiritual and eternal blessings which belong to such. He that prefers his own ease and safety in this world to the truths, the service, and the institutions of Christ, cannot be justly deemed one that sincerely loves Him, or one to whom He is precious.

The same lesson of instruction is taught us by the parable of the treasure hid in a field, which, when a man has found, he goeth, and selleth all that he hath, and buyeth that field. And likewise by that of a merchant-man, seeking goodly pearls, who having found one pearl of great price, goes and parts with all, that he may be possessed of that pearl. He is willing to give up the riches, the honours and pleasures of this world, for the enjoyment of that inestimable treasure which he has discovered. Now to have a heart to forsake all for Christ, is the same thing, in effect, as actually doing it, so far as there is occasion, and so far as we are put to the trial. What our Lord speaks of "selling all that we have," is to be understood of a disposition of mind to be ready and prepared to do it, if it be necessary. Many of the primitive Christians shewed their regard for the Saviour and His followers, by actually doing this, though their example is no farther binding upon us, than as it relates to that disposition of mind which all the followers of Jesus should possess, namely, a readiness to part with all for His sake, whenever there is a proper call to it.

Self-denial, in respect to things in themselves sinful, should be universal, otherwise we do not give proper evidence of the sincerity of our regard for Christ. Many go very far in a profession of religion, and yet live in the habitual indulgence of some sin, either great or small, secret or open. Judas made so fair a shew, that all the other disciples questioned their own sincerity rather than his. Yet Judas was covetous. Herod was a hearer of John the Baptist, nay, heard him gladly, and did many things which John recommended; yet Herod was resolved to live in incest. It is the same in many other cases. O reader, examine yourself, and beware of splitting upon this rock. If your heart is not sound in the statutes of heaven, you are in danger of being put to shame another day.

Let us labour then, to mortify corrupt affections, and not wilfully indulge ourselves in any ill habit, custom, or practice. Without habitually resigning ourselves to God, and labouring to subdue irregular passions and inclinations, supposing we are real Christians, we cannot expect our souls to prosper in the use of the means of grace. If Agag be spared, from whatever motive, our sacrifices, like those of Saul, will neither be acceptable to God, nor profitable to ourselves.

Satan and sin unite their art
To keep me from my Lord:
Dear Saviour, guard my trembling heart,
And guide me by Thy word.

The path to Thy divine abode
Through a wide desert lies;
A thousand snares beset the road,
A thousand dangers rise.

Whene'er the tempting foe alarms,
Or spreads the fatal snare,
I'll fly to my Redeemer's arms,
For safety must be there.

Dear Lord, obedient to Thy call,
I would the world resign,
Deny myself, give up my all,
And be for ever Thine.

SECTION 9

IF CHRIST IS PRECIOUS TO US, WE SHALL BE DISTRESSED THAT WE ARE NOT MORE CONFRMED TO HIS BLESSED IMAGE AND HOLY WILL.

In proportion as He is precious to us, will be our aversion to sin and all unholiness. In the undertakings, the sufferings, and the death of our Redeemer for us, we have such a representation of the evil of sin, and of the dreadful punishment due to it, as must tend to inspire our hearts with hatred against it.

We see in the wounds, the sorrows, and the crucifixion of the Saviour, the dreadful malignity of sin. We see how hateful it is to God, since He punished it so severely in His beloved Son, when in our room, He bare it in His own body on the tree. We read the nature of sin, in characters of blood, on the cross of Christ. All the laboured declamations of moralists on the intrinsic deformity of vice, can never represent it in such proper colours as it is seen here.

Those who have a due sense of the spirituality of the divine law, and who strictly examine their own hearts and lives by that perfect rule of righteousness, will ever see abundant reason for humiliation and self-abasement before God.

From love to Jesus Christ will arise, hatred of those things which are contrary to His will, and which oppose and hinder us in our endeavours after conformity to Him. The vain imaginations of our own evil hearts will be matter of grief and sorrow to us, "I hate vain thoughts, but Thy law do I love."

The Christian is grieved and distressed that His thoughts and affections are so much exercised concerning the affairs of the present life, and that he should be so insensible and unmoved at many times, in respect to the affairs of another world; that his heart should be so hard, so dull and unaffected about matters of infinite moment. He mourns to think that his love to God is so cold, that his desires after Him are so languid, that his zeal for Him is so low, and his gratitude for favours received so small.

His heart is pained within him that he should feel himself so insensible and unmoved under the sound of the gospel. That he should sit and hear of the astonishing love of God in Christ Jesus, and of His giving His beloved Son to bleed and die for our sins, without being melted into penitence, and inspired with love and zeal. That he should be so unaffected with the amazing kindness and compassion of Jesus Christ, manifested in His dying agonies, His bloody sweat, His ignominious cross, His loud and bitter cries, His pierced side, and bleeding heart, and all this for His bitter enemies, to deliver them from deserved and eternal destruction, and to bring them to the possession of everlasting glory and felicity. "Surely," says he, "if there is a call for the exercise of fervent affections any where, it is here at the foot of the cross. O how I am disquieted to think that I should be so stupid and insensible, even when I could wish my heart to be most engaged! Can any thing be presented to my thoughts more important, more wonderful, or more interesting? And yet how superficial and inefficacious, at some times, are the impressions which are made upon my mind by these views!

"Blessed Jesus! How cold, how feeble, how languid is my love to Thee, who art altogether lovely. Alas! How readily are my fluctuating passions captivated by the objects of sense! O that I might feel the force of that motive, of loving Him who hath first loved me! May Thy love, O precious Saviour, constrain me, and attach me intimately to Thyself when I consider what Thou hast done for me. Do Thou, by a gentle but powerful influence, attract my desires. Though mine eyes have never seen Thy lovely face, though no accent of Thy voice has reached my ear, yet Thou canst make Thyself more intimate to my soul, than any of the objects of sense. O let me not live so estranged from Thee. Warm my cold, and frozen heart, and kindle up in my bosom a flame of holy fervour towards Thee.

"Keep me, O my God, in every hour of temptation. Unsupported by Thy preventing hand I fall, I wound my conscience, and dishonour Thy name. But, armed with Thy protection, I shall stand fast, be strong, and victorious. O strengthen me to war a good warfare, that at length I may overcome, through Him that hath loved me. Be at my right hand to save me, lest the enemy should triumph over me, and I be made the reproach of the foolish. I dread the thought of being left to myself. In the hour of temptation I have a thousand times experienced my own weakness and inconstancy. Every divine impression has seemed to be obliterated. The celestial scenes which before engaged my attention have disappeared; paradise, and the glories of the skies, have fled like an airy vision; and the most important truths of Christianity have been concealed from my view, as if I had never known them. Lord, what is man! My soul is humbled within me because of my foolishness."

At some seasons, the believer's mind is so oppressed with a sense of his own vileness, that he is ready to sink into despondency and dejection. In his retired moments he pours out his complaints in such language as this: "The clogs of guilt and the clouds of darkness hang heavy on my soul. What language can express the depth of my distress on account of sin! The spirit of a man may sustain his infirmities; but a wounded spirit who can bear? A sense of the vilest ingratitude to the best of Beings stings my conscious bosom, and deprives me of repose. All is gloomy within; all is discouragement without. What returns have I made for favours received? I cannot bear the sight of my own vileness. I abhor myself, and repent as in dust and ashes. The several periods of my life have been marked with repeated instances of ingratitude to Him, who is the giver of every good and perfect gift, whom I desire to love, and to obey with my whole heart. My unstable soul has been perpetually starting aside from God, inclining to folly, and verging towards that which is evil. This, this is wretchedness indeed. For this I condemn myself almost without ceasing. My spirits droop, my heart desponds, my soul is disquieted within me. Lord, be merciful to me, pardon mine iniquity, for it is great!" Yet, amidst these gloomy, these self-condemning thoughts, light sometimes breaks in upon the mind, and then

—*The humble Christian feels within*
A spring of consolation from above,
And secret cordials, which repair his strength,
Raise and uphold his fainting, languid heart.

Among the many considerations which excite the believer's sorrow for the evil propensities of his mind, and the miscarriages of his life, that of the Redeemer's death for his offences is not the least efficacious. To think of the love of Jesus to my poor soul, manifested in His sorrows, His sufferings, His agonies, and the shedding of His precious blood, penetrates my heart, and makes me loathe myself in my own sight. While I look to Him upon the cross whom I have pierced by my offences, surely I ought to mourn, and be in bitterness, as one that mourneth for his first-born. Shall not I shed tears of grief for those sins, for which my Redeemer shed His precious blood!

It is true, the constitutions of men are different, some have tears at command, and others can scarcely weep on any occasion. But the want of tears, should in this case, be made up by inward grief. Yet I must beg leave to say, that if men can shed tears on lighter occasions (and all the causes of sorrow are light in comparison with this) but never shed a tear on account of their ingratitude to a dying Saviour, it seems to indicate a want of love to Him, and that they have not a just sense of the evil and malignity of sin. The penitent woman, mentioned in the gospel, sat at the feet of Jesus weeping; she washed His feet with her tears, and wiped them with the hair of her head.

"Break, break, O thou insensible heart! And ye mine eyes, why are ye not fountains of tears, that I might weep day and night? Lord, I abhor myself on account of the defilement which cleaveth unto me. Behold I am vile, I will lay my hand upon my mouth, and put my face in the dust. I have experienced a thousand proofs of Thy goodness, the remembrance of which fills me with confusion, because of my ingratitude. I cannot in any instance charge Thee with severity. Thy laws are not rigorous or grievous, but holy just and good. And yet I have frequently violated the sacred rules which my heart approves. But the height of my folly lies, in having so often sinned against infinite goodness and love. I have abused

Thy kindness, and affronted Thy clemency. O Lord, I beseech Thee pardon mine iniquity, for it is great."

Such exercises of mind as these, strongly indicate the sincerity of our regard for the divine Saviour.

Alas! how wide my spirit flies,
And wanders from her God!
My soul forgets her heavenly prize,
And treads the downward road.

How my wild passions rage within,
Nor Thy commands obey;
And flesh and sense enslav'd to sin,
Draw my best thoughts away.

Shall creatures of a meaner frame
Pay all their dues to Thee;
Creatures which never knew Thy name,
Nor ever lov'd like me?

Great God! create my soul anew,
Conform my heart to Thine;
Melt down my will, and let it flow,
And take the mould divine.

Then shall my feet no more depart,
No more my senses rove;
Devotion shall be all my heart,
And all my passions love.

SECTION 10

IF CHRIST IS PRECIOUS TO US, WE SHALL ADHER TO HIM IN ALL CONDITIONS.

We shall persevere in His ways and service, amidst all the various trials with which we may be exercised. If persons who make a profession of religion live any considerable time in this world of affliction and trouble, they must meet with many trials of their sincerity and steadfastness. It evidently appears from the sacred Scriptures, that the all-wise God designedly brings His children into a state of trial and difficulty for their good; and particularly that it may be made manifest to themselves and others, that they belong to Him, by their being enabled to endure this course of severe discipline, without fainting in the day of adversity.[21]

After the patriarch Abraham had stood his ground amidst many other sharp exercises, it pleased God, towards the close of his life, to tempt, or try him, by giving him that singular and awful command, to take his only son Isaac, whom he loved, and to offer him up for a burnt sacrifice. Abraham fully demonstrated the sincerity and strength of his faith by his readiness to obey this mysterious injunction.

When the children of Israel had nothing to drink but the bitter waters of Marah, it is said that there "the Lord proved them." Their being destitute of provisions for the support of life was to answer the same end; till at length, in their greatest extremity of distress, the Lord said unto Moses, "Behold, I will rain bread from heaven for you." He afterwards told them, that the design of their being led through the wilderness for the space of forty years, was to humble them, to prove them, and to know what was in their hearts, whether they would keep His commandments or not. The wilderness was great and terrible, wherein were fiery serpents, and scorpions, and drought; where there was no water to supply them but what was "brought out of the flinty rock." The Lord thus dealt

---

21 *Justin Martyr*, addressing himself to the emperor and the senate of Rome, says, "Our Master, Jesus Christ, from whom we take the name of Christians, the Son and messenger of that God who is the supreme Lord and maker of the universe, has foretold our sufferings; which to us is a manifest confirmation of all His other doctrines, because we see these things fulfilled according to His prediction. For this or nothing is the work of God, to declare that a thing shall come to pass long before it is in being, and then to bring about that thing, according to the same declaration."—*Justin Martyr* Apol. Pro. Christ. xiv.

with them, not from a want of regard to them, but as He repeatedly declared, for the purpose of trying them, that "He might do them good in their latter end. For the Lord your God proveth you to know whether ye love Him with all your heart, and with all your soul."

When they were settled in the land of promise, the Lord said to them, "I will not henceforth drive out the nations which Joshua left when he died, that through them I may prove Israel, whether they will keep the way of the Lord, to walk therein, or not." Some such method as this God is pleased to take with His spiritual Israel in all ages.

We have a very singular and instructive instance of the end and use of adversity, in the case of Job. That holy man was severely tried; yet, in the depth of His calamity, we hear him say, "My foot hath held His steps; His way have I kept, and not declined; neither have I gone back from the commandment of His lips. I have esteemed the words of His mouth more than my necessary food. Though He slay me, yet will I trust in Him. He knoweth the way that I take; when He hath tried me, I shall come forth as gold."

Now, the man is blessed that endureth temptation; the issue will be glorious; for when he is tried, he shall receive the crown of life. We are therefore admonished not to think it strange concerning the fiery trial which is to try us, as though some strange thing happened unto us. By our steady adherence to Christ and His cause in the midst of all, we have the fairest opportunity given us, of proving how precious He is to our souls.

True Christians have such views of the transcendent excellency of the Redeemer, that they are powerfully drawn after Him, and attached to Him in all conditions of life into which they may be brought. They see Him worthy to be followed, though they should be called to forsake all for Him, and to endure the severest persecutions for His sake. Others, in time of temptation, fall away. But they endure the storm, for the love which they bear to His name. Through the views which they have of His superlative amiableness and excellency, they are thoroughly disposed to be subject to Him, and engaged to labour with earnestness and activity in His service, amidst all the difficulties, trials, and troubles which they may must with in so doing. It is the discovery of His divine excellency which makes them constant to Him; for this so deeply impresses their minds, that they cannot forget or forsake Him. They will follow Him wheresoever He goeth, and the solicitations and the persecutions of men, and the guile and malice of Satan are employed in vain to draw them away from Him.

Some "have had trial of cruel mockings and scourgings, yea, moreover, of bonds and imprisonments. They were stoned, they were sawn asunder, were tempted, were slain with the sword: they wandered about in sheep skins, and goat skins; being destitute, afflicted, tormented; of whom the world was not worthy; they wandered in deserts, and in mountains, and in dens and caves of the earth." Yet all could not wean their hearts from Jesus, nor extinguish their love to Him. They were enabled to maintain their attachment to Him in the midst of all, because He was precious to their souls.

SECTION 11

IF CHRIST BE PRECIOUS UNTO US, WE SHALL BE CONCERNED TO MAKE HIS GLORY THE END OF OUR ACTIONS.

Our blessed Lord died, as the substitute of sinners, that those who live by His death should not live unto themselves, making their own honour, ease, or pleasure, the end of their living in this world; but that they should devote their lives to the service, the interest, and the glory of their great Lord and Saviour, who died in their room, to take away their sins by the sacrifice of Himself, and who rose again for their justification.

We have a lively exemplification of this in the apostle Paul. When a prisoner at Rome, he wrote to the brethren at Philippi, to establish them in the truth which they had received, and to exhort them not to be shaken in mind by the persecutions which he endured; for he was persuaded these would, in the issue, be for the furtherance of the gospel. "According," says he, "to my earnest expectation and my hope, that in nothing I shall be ashamed, but that with all boldness, as always so now also, Christ shall be magnified in my body, whether it be by life or by death." He then adds, "For to me to live is Christ, and to die is gain." As if he had said, "I have expressed my hope that Christ shall be glorified in me, whether I die or live, and in this hope I am encouraged, because He is the supreme end of my life. I value life only as it may be employed to the purpose of His honour. The interest and the glory of my Redeemer are the great ends I pursue, with unabating ardour and delight; that in publishing His blessed gospel, and suffering for His sake, I may gain over souls to Him, and so promote His honour in the world."

As the life of a Christian is derived from Christ, so it is directed to Him. It is most certain, that, when he is actuated by the noble principles which the gospel inspires, the honour of his Saviour's name, and the advancement of religion, lie nearest his heart. And this seems to be the special import of the words above recited, from the connection in which they stand, "To me to live is Christ;"—"he is all and in all to me; I live only for Him."

The whole of the apostle's life serves to illustrate this declaration. In the midst of shame, hunger, nakedness, bonds, and imprisonment, he was happy if his Lord and Master might be honoured thereby. He counted not his life dear unto himself, so that he might finish his course with joy, and the ministry which he had received of the Lord Jesus, to testify the gospel of the grace of God. When his friends endeavoured to dissuade him from going to Jerusalem, because of the dangers to which he would be exposed in that city, he said, "What mean ye to weep and to break my heart? I am ready, not only to be bound, but to die at Jerusalem, for the name of the Lord Jesus."

This heavenly man lived and breathed only for the honour of the Redeemer, and for the advancement of his kingdom in the world. The Jews hated him to rage and madness. The Gentiles threatened him, sought his life, and persecuted him in the different places where Divine Providence sent him. When at Rome, in the hands of Nero, as in the paws of a raging lion, he was tranquil and serene; concerned for nothing so much as the honour of Christ. Whence was that calmness of mind which he invariably discovered on such occasions? Was his heart of iron or steel? Was he insensible to the troubles which agitate other men? No; he was no stoic. His soul was all tenderness and sensibility. But a supreme regard to Christ carried him above all. The Saviour's love constrained him. Jesus was precious unto him. Where his honour was in question, he would neither be influenced by the desire of life, nor the dread of death. A regard for the glory of his Divine Master overcame all. Noble spirit! This is Christian heroism in all its sublimity; infinitely superior to the brutal ferocity of your Alexanders and your Caesars. Their only aim was to aggrandize themselves, though this should be done by cruelty and oppression. The highest wish of this blessed apostle was, to glorify the Redeemer, in promoting the welfare, the liberty and happiness of those whom He died to save.

But it is not enough to admire so fine an example we ought in our inferior stations, so far as we are able, to copy after it. We know who has repeatedly told us, that unless we prefer Him to all that is dear to us in this world, we cannot be His disciples. The steady and reigning design of our souls should be, that we may live to Christ, and make His honour the end of all our actions. We should count our services, our exertions, our labours, and even our sufferings delightful, if this end may be any way promoted by them. All we possess should be consecrated to Him who gave Himself for us. The members of our bodies, and the faculties of our souls should be employed for Him. Our tongues should speak His praises, our ears should hearken to His voice, our eyes should review His wonderful works, our feet should run in His ways, and our hands should be employed in the execution of every thing in our power, which is pleasing in His sight. In all places, in all companies, in every undertaking, civil or religious, it should be our aim to glorify Him. The general rule laid down by the apostle Paul, should be always kept in remembrance, "Whether ye eat or drink, or whatsoever ye do, do all to the glory of God;" and in another place, he speaks much to the same purpose, "Whatsoever ye do, in word or deed, do all in the name of the Lord Jesus, giving thanks to God the Father by Him."

We should never forget that we are not our own, but are bought with a price, for this very end, that we should glorify God with our bodies, and with our spirits which are His. All the operations of His grace upon us are for the same purpose, that we should shew forth the virtues and the praise of Him who hath called us out of darkness into the marvelous light. This will be our delightful employ through the revolutions of a blissful eternity. That Jesus who is precious to us has said, "If any man serve Me, him will My Father honour;" and surely those who expect to be glorified with Him in heaven, should make it their business, their aim, and their constant endeavour to glorify Him upon earth. To present our bodies, together with our souls to Him, a living sacrifice, holy and acceptable in His sight, is a reasonable service.

It grieves me, Lord, it grieves me sore,
That I have lived to Thee no more,
And wasted half my days;
My inward powers shall burn and flame
With glowing zeal for Thy great name,
I would not speak, but for my God,
Nor move, but to His praise.

SECTION 12

IF CHRIST IS PRECIOUS TO US, WE SHALL LONG TO BE WITH HIM.

We shall not only entertain joyful hopes of future felicity, but we shall live, in expectation of the promised inheritance. We shall feel, at certain seasons, ardent desires of seeing Him upon His throne of glory, to whose humiliation, agonies and death, we are indebted for all our salvation. We shall wish to join the happy society who, without ceasing, celebrate His praise, crying, "Worthy is the Lamb that was slain, to receive power, and riches, and wisdom, and strength, and honour, and glory, and blessing; for He hath redeemed us to God by His blood."

The weather-beaten traveller longs to be at home, that he may enjoy the company of those who are most dear to him. The mariner, after having been exposed to many storms and tempests, in a long and dangerous voyage, longs to reach the port of rest. The desired haven is much in His thoughts, and the nearer he approaches it, the more constantly and ardently he looks out for it. So longs the believing soul to be in the immediate presence of Him, whom having not seen he loves.

"The hearts of believers," says the judicious Dr. Owen, "are like the needle, which cannot rest till it comes to the point to which it is directed, by the mysterious virtue of the magnet. For being once touched by the love of Christ, and receiving from it an impression of secret, ineffable virtue, they will ever be in motion, and restless, until they come to Him, and behold His glory. That soul which can be satisfied with it, has neither part nor lot in the matter."

"I have waited," says the Christian, "for Thy salvation, O Lord; when wilt Thou admit me into Thy holy habitation? How long shall I lie at this distance from Thee?"

Whoever considers what it is to behold the glorious face of Jesus in heaven, to contemplate a beauty which never fades, to be enriched with a beneficence which can never be exhausted, and blessed in a love which is unmerited and infinite, will find abundant reason to say again and again, "I have a desire to depart, and be with Christ." "Why is the time of my absence from Him prolonged? When shall the days of my pilgrimage have an end? When shall I see the face of my Redeemer, without a veil between? Many of my friends are gone before me; and now, secure of the conquest over all their enemies, they possess the rewards of victory, and are triumphing in the regions of immortality. They survey what was once to them the field of contest, and look back with unutterable pleasure on the dangers which are now past. Their united foes are for ever vanquished, and they inherit uninterrupted tranquillity and repose. Their eyes behold the King in His beauty. They are in His presence where there is fulness of joy, and at His right hand where there are pleasures for evermore. O how I long to join their blessed society, Come, Lord Jesus, come quickly! This must be the language of my soul, till the solemn, the sweet moment of Thy appearance arrive."

Supposing we were to have no pleasure on this side heaven, yet the prospect of being happy there to all eternity, should teach us to be calm and patient under every calamity here, and even to bear these light afflictions, which are but for a moment, with a holy joy. There we shall see Jesus, live with Him, and enjoy the glorious light of His countenance, not for a day, a month, an age, but for ever. And who can tell the pleasure, peace, joy, and transport of a glorified saint, in the immediate presence of His ever-adorable and all-gracious Redeemer? When he is admitted into His glorious palace above the skies, with what surprise and astonishment must he be seized? We can conceive but very imperfectly of the first impressions made upon him by the objects into the midst of which he finds himself transported. He there sees multitudes of all nations, countries, and languages, uniting in the admiration of infinite love, casting themselves before the throne of God, laying their crowns at His feet, and crying, from the abundance of a heart penetrated with the perfection of a Being so worthy of their homage and adoration, "Blessing, and glory, and honour to Him that sitteth upon the throne, and to the Lamb for ever and ever." May we not suppose such a newly arrived inhabitant of the celestial place to say within himself, "Is this heaven, and am I here?"

It is described to us by a variety of figures, and metaphorical expressions. We judge of happiness and misery, according to what we are conversant with in the present state. But in a future state, the veils of flesh and blood shall be taken away. The darkness which now beclouds our minds will be dispelled, and all the scales of ignorance will fall from our eyes. We shall no more see as through a glass darkly, but face to face. Then we shall know what is meant by the marriage-supper of the Lamb, and by sitting down with Abraham, Isaac, and Jacob in the kingdom of God.

There are angels, archangels, cherubim and seraphim, thrones, dominions, princedoms, virtues, powers; the general assembly and church of the first-born; there are patriarchs. prophets, apostles, and martyrs; there are myriads of saints, a great multitude which no man can number; there the throne of glory, the fulness of joy, the rivers of pure and everlasting delight, the pleasures which flow from God's right hand for evermore. The departing saint no sooner quits His earthly tabernacle, than he mingles with the morning stars, and engages in familiar converse with the first-born sons of light. The supreme excellence unveils itself, and suffers him to gaze on infinite beauty. The Lord of nature, the Being of beings displays there the bright assemblage of His adorable perfections. There is the eternal father; there the wellbeloved Son, clothed in a body like our own; and there the blessed Spirit.

The Christian longs to be in heaven upon many accounts; but chiefly, that he may see and enjoy his God without interruption; next to this, that he may for ever be favoured with the blessed communion of saints. When he lays aside his frail garments of mortality, he is clothed with the white robes of purity, glory, and honour. He immediately feels the force, and breathes the raptures of immortal love. The smiling moments, crowned with joy and ever-blooming life, now begin their everlasting round.

The believing prospect of future glory is the great persuasive to holy obedience, and constant patience under the trials of life; since noting can be too much to do or to suffer, in the view of that blessed state. How happy is the condition of the man who waits, with firmness and steadiness, for that crown of glory to which he has a clear and certain right! Who can draw from a well-grounded hope of it, pleasures suitable to an intelligent creature, and an immortal soul! Who, in the midst of so many pains, so many miseries, so many labours with which this mortal life abounds, feels in his bosom that source of consolation which is connected with a firm expectation of eternal felicity! How is he fortified against the terrors of death! Death to him is disarmed of its sting, and the grave of its boasted victory. What can we wish more suited to our circumstances in these regions of mortality, than to know that our Redeemer lives, and that we shall presently live with Him, where death shall be known no more!

To an impenitent sinner death appears as the messenger of God's vengeance, who comes to lead him to that tribunal where all his crimes will be examined and punished. When that awful moment arrives, the blandishments of the world vanish like a dream; a gathering gloom veils the face of nature, and eclipses all its beauty. No created enjoyment can cheer the sullen hours, while he stands shivering on the brink of an unknown, unfathomable eternity. These solemnities are new to him, and infinitely more awful than he had ever imagined. The king of terrors stands insulting before him, and draws his sable curtain round the bed of languishing.

The time of our abode in this transitory world is very uncertain, and the final event of things very awful and important. The ancient heathens, to avoid the thought of death, forbore to mention the very name of it. And as it was impossible to live upon earth without having occasion to speak of the end of life, they expressed by a *periphrasis* that which they were so reluctant to name. Instead of calling it death, they termed it a submitting to destiny, a falling by the stroke of fate, a departing, and a sleeping; but to change the name of a frightful object will not much diminish the horror of it. The two expressions last mentioned are adopted, and, at the same time, sanctified by the inspired writers. *Paul* speaks, with holy tranquillity, of the time of his departure being at hand. And death is called a sleep, as it is, to a good man, the period of his entering into rest. And it has this name given it with a peculiar respect to the resurrection, when they that sleep in the dust of the earth shall awake, and arise, some to everlasting life, and some to shame and everlasting contempt.

May I have that love for Jesus which will render it a desirable object to depart, that I may be for ever with Him! This is the only way to die with comfort. May the great purposes of life be answered in me, and at length the hour of death be welcomed with cheerfulness, that I may then have nothing to do but to resign my spirit into the hands of my Saviour. I shall then bid adieu to this tenement of clay, to have no farther connection with it, till the course of nature be dissolved, and the sun have measured his last radiant circle round the skies. It requires something more than human fortitude to support the soul under the immediate views of this separation. Here the resolution of nature and the aids of reason fail.

> But faith can triumph o'er the grave,
> And trample on the tombs;
> My Jesus, my Redeemer lives,
> My God, my Saviour comes.

Then, O my soul, thy deliverance will be complete from all that now infetters thee. My bonds will fall off; I shall be perfectly free from all the snares of sense and sin which have formerly entangled me. I shall be oppressed with no weights, held down by no clogs of guilt, weakness or affliction. My whole soul, and my body too, after the great rising day, will enjoy the glorious liberty of the children of God. How unspeakable will be the pleasure of having every faculty and affection at command, and of having the free exercise of all! When the poor prisoner has his fetters knocked off, and full liberty is given him to quit his loathsome dungeon, and breathe the free air, how great is his joy! The bird escaped from confinement, claps its wings, and with alacrity takes its aerial flight. This is a faint emblem of the joy I shall feel, when mortality shall be swallowed up of life. The language of the happy society will be in that day, "Our soul is escaped as a bird out of the snare of the fowler; the snare is broken, and we are escaped. They will then feel themselves free from all confinement, and no longer say, "When we would do good, evil is present with us."

My soul is winged with fervent desire after the bright vision of my Saviour's face, and intensely longs for her dismission from the regions of mortality. Oh, when shall the important period arrive! I sigh for permission to enter the world of perfect light and love. I am still in a state of warfare; yet various as the sources of suffering are, the conflict, in which I am supported by the hope of future rest, can neither be long nor altogether painful. The great object of my expectation cannot be very far distant. A few years, a few months, nay, even a few days may bring me into that state of being, where the Fountain of everlasting light displays His glories, and where neither clouds nor darkness can ever intercept His radiant brightness. I long, with increasing desire, that indulgent Heaven would sign my release, and speedily dismiss me from this scene of combat. When shall the storms of life be past? When shall I reach the haven where I would be? When shall I enter the regions of perfect light and felicity, the paradise of God, where stands the tree of life, and where an unbounded spring, in all its glory, for ever, ever blooms?

Come, blessed angel, raise my soul
To this divine abode;
Haste, for my spirit longs to see
My Saviour and my God.

Chapter Four

In What Respects Jesus Christ Is Precious To Them That Believe

To you that believe, He is *precious*, or He is your honour. You account Him your glory and your gain. He is not only precious to you, but *preciousness* itself. He is your jewel, your treasure; and should you be robbed of all besides, in Him you are superlatively and everlastingly rich. By the faith which you have in His name, you are enabled to discern His excellency, who is fairer than the children of men, nay, the chiefest among ten thousands, and altogether lovely. As such you must account Him precious, and bestow the choicest affections of your hearts upon Him. If the question is proposed to you, "What is thy Beloved more than another beloved?" you will not be at a loss for an answer. He is precious in every view, and under every consideration. All that is in Him, all that is done or spoken by Him, and all that appertains to Him is precious. Let us enumerate a few particulars, by way of illustration.

SECTION 1

THE HISTORY OF CHRIST IS PRECIOUS TO THEM THAT BELIEVE.

This is given us by the four evangelists, under the immediate inspiration of the Holy Spirit. They have related every material circumstance concerning the birth, the life, the sufferings, the death, the resurrection, and the ascension of Jesus Christ, in a manner so simple, so artless, and yet so sublime, as must captivate the attention, and touch the heart of every unprejudiced reader. The facts they record are the most interesting that ever employed the historic pen.

The incarnation of the Saviour of mankind was one of the most important, one of the most glorious events that ever took place in the revolutions of time. Then the virgin conceived and brought forth a Son, whose name is *God with us*. The Lord of glory took up His dwelling in mortal flesh. The purposes and promises of God relating to this wonderful transaction were then fulfilled. The fulness of the times was then completed, and God sent forth His Son made of a woman. Angels descended from heaven to bring the joyful news. A multitude of the heavenly host made their appearance on the occasion. Celestial music was heard by mortal ears. The glorious messengers had no sooner delivered the glad tidings, than they united in one of the anthems of heaven. The morning stars sang together, and the sons of God shouted for joy; "Glory to God in the highest, and on earth, peace, goodwill towards men."[22] The Son of Righteousness was now to arise

---

22   A certain writer enumerates the circumstances attending the Saviour's birth in the following animated manner, "*Herod* turns pale on his throne: the powers of darkness tremble; the eastern sages suspend their speculations, and attend to no sign in the firmament excepting that which conducts them to the new-born Saviour. A minister of light is the herald of the astonishing event, and cries to the wakeful shepherds, who mingled their midnight devotions with their care for

and shine upon a benighted world, and a new star appeared in the heavens, as a signal of this brighter day. Wise men from the east, taught of God to know the significancy of this sacred token, came, under the guidance of its shining rays, to present their gifts, and pay their adorations to the new-born Saviour. Such is the history of His birth. Abraham, the patriarch, rejoiced in the distant prospect of this day; he saw it by faith, and was glad.

The account given us of the public life and ministry of Jesus is precious. His entrance on the important work He had to do, was signalized by the manifestation of the glorious Trinity. When He was baptized of John in Jordan, He went up straightway out of the water; and lo, the heavens were opened unto Him, and John saw the Spirit of God descending like a dove, and lighting upon Him: and lo, a voice from heaven, saying, "This is My beloved Son, in whom I am well pleased." After His harbinger had directed the sinful multitude, who surrounded His person, to behold Him as the Lamb of God which taketh away the sin of the world, Jesus began to preach the glad tidings of the kingdom, and to confirm His divine mission by a vast variety of astonishing miracles. He went about doing good, and healing all that were diseased. The blind received their sight, the lame were made to walk, the dumb to speak, the deaf to hear; demons were expelled from those who had been tormented by them; those who were sick of the palsy were restored to the perfect use of their limbs; the lepers were

---

their flocks, 'Behold, I bring you glad tidings of great joy, which shall be unto all people; for unto you is born this day, in the city of *David*, a Saviour, which is Christ the Lord.' And straightway, a multitude of the heavenly host congratulate the shepherds, on the Son of God's assumption of mortal flesh.

The celestial spirits wondered to behold their Creator and Lord become a Babe at *Bethlehem*, wrapped in swaddling clothes, and laid in a manger. From the moment of His nativity, how deep were His humiliation and abasement! Yet in that inglorious place where oxen fed, the heavenly hosts adore Him. The Magi paid divine honours to the incarnate God. His presence consecrated the stable into a temple of glory, and ennobled the manger where He lay, so as to make it in some sort, a throne of grace."

cleansed, and even the dead were called back to life, by His omnipotent word.

This was the day for which the church of God had looked and longed, for the space of almost four thousand years. Patriarchs, prophets, and kings had waited for it, with earnest expectation. Now it was come. The glory of the Lord was revealed; the Only Begotten of the Father, full of grace and truth, was made manifest. The greatest honour was conferred on this earthly globe at that period, when He who formed it by His almighty power became its inhabitant. The glory of the second temple was greater than that of the first, because the Son of God Himself made His appearance in it. If a poor man should be favoured with the presence of a prince, or an emperor under the roof of his cottage, he would think it a great honour. What an honour then was conferred on this world, when the King of Glory became its inhabitant!

The sojourning of the Son of God on earth, is the chief event which adorns the records of time, and enlivens the history of the world. It is the glory of the air that He breathed in it; of the sun, that its beams once shone upon Him; of the ground, that He trod upon it; and of the sea, that He walked serenely on its glassy surface. It is the glory of the elements, that they once nourished Him who is the bread of life; of the water, that it quenched his thirst; of men, that He lived among them; and of Judea, that it was the land of Immanuel, where He sojourned more than thirty years. It is the glory of our nature that He assumed it, and, by so doing, exalted it to a high degree.

The dispensations of Providence, through successive ages, like so many lines, point at this period, as their centre. Before His appearance, they made way for His coming; and since that period, they are subservient to the great ends to be answered by it. The history of His sufferings and death is equally interesting, and equally precious. That He should suffer, bleed, and die, was the design of the Father in sending Him into the world. The Spirit of God, in the ancient prophets, signified beforehand, the sufferings of Christ, and the glory that should follow.

Led by the sacred historians, let this solemn and affecting scene employ my meditation. Think, O my soul, on that most tragical, and yet most glorious event, on which thy salvation depends. Call to mind the astonishing, the almost incredible history of thy Saviour's love. He who upholdeth all things by the word of His power, who thought it no robbery to be equal with God, humbled Himself so as to become obedient unto death, even the death of the cross. Behold Him loaded with those sorrows which He willingly bore for our sakes. Follow Him into the garden of Gethsemane; see the awful combat which He there sustained; a combat in which He defended Himself only by His prayers, His cries, and His tears; a combat which led on to something still more formidable, the very thought of which so overwhelmed His holy soul, that His sweat was as it were great drops of blood falling down to the ground, and He cried out, "Father, if it be possible, let this cup pass from me."

Let me proceed still farther, and review that torrent of sufferings which the adorable Redeemer endured, from the period of His being led away out of the garden by a band of ruffians, to the hour of His crucifixion. Behold Him accused by the loud clamour of a thousand revengeful and blaspheming tongues. Hear the fatal sentence pronounced against Him by a prevaricating judge, who declared, that he believed Him to be perfectly innocent. See His lovely visage marred, His face defiled with spitting; His hands bound with cords; His temples crowned with pricking thorns; His body bruised with rude blows, and His back scourged with rods, till they might tell all His bones. See Him, after all this, trembling under the weight of that cross on which He was to expire, in agonies which cannot be described. Ascend with Him to the place of skulls, the theatre of the greatest wonders which omnipotence itself ever wrought!

Behold there the Lamb of God! Behold that Jesus, who is the brightness of His Father's glory, and the express image of His person; see Him stripped of His garments, nailed to the infamous gibbet, treated as the vilest malefactors, and, during that awful period, having, as it were, lost sight of those favourable regards of His divine Father, which constituted all His joy. Hear Him, hear Him crying out, "My God, My God, why hast Thou forsaken Me!"

Nature was thrown into convulsions. The earth quaked. Rocks were rent. The heavens were clad in mourning. The very graves being opened resigned their prey, and many of them that slept arose and showed themselves alive after His passion. On this great day, for which all other days were made, atonement was offered up for human guilt; awful, avenging justice, which called for our blood, was fully and completely satisfied; the price was paid for the ransom of our souls; eternal redemption was obtained; our old man was crucified, that the body of sin might be destroyed; principalities and powers were conquered; the world was overcome; death and the grave were subdued; the eternal law of God, which we had violated, was magnified and made honourable; and all the attributes of Deity were infinitely glorified.

The justice of God is glorified by the punishment of impenitent sinners in hell, His goodness by the happiness of saints in heaven. But the death of Christ glorifies them both in a degree unspeakably higher. In this divine expedient, mercy and truth meet together, righteousness and peace embrace each other. By consequence, a way is opened for the communication of every blessing, which we, perishing sinners, stand in need of, to make us completely and everlastingly happy. Pardon, peace, justification, acceptance, perseverance, and eternal life are all ensured by the Saviour's death. The wretchedness of that state, out of which we are delivered, can only be equalled by the blessedness of that into which we are brought, by our dying Redeemer.

With joy, with grief, the healing hand I see;
Ah! too conspicuous! it is fix'd on high.
On high?—kind Heav'n forgive the erring muse;
Alas, how low! how far beneath the skies!
The skies it form'd, yet now it bleeds for me—
Draw the dire steel—Ah no! the dreadful blessing
What heart, or can sustain, or dares forego?
There hangs all human hope: that nail supports
The falling universe: that gone, we sink.
He seiz'd our dreadful right; the load sustain'd;
And heav'd the mountain from a guilty world.
A thousand worlds, so bought, were bought too dear.
The theme is all divine: my heart! awake!
What can awake thee, unawak'd by this,
Expended Deity on human weal?

The sun beheld it—No, the shocking scene
Drove back His chariot: midnight veil'd His face,
A midnight nature shudder'd to behold.
Sun! didst thou fly thy Maker's pain? or start
At that enormous load of human guilt,
Which bow'd His blessed head; o'erwhelm'd His cross;
Made green the centre; burst earth's marble womb,
With pangs, strange pangs! deliver'd of her dead?
Hell howl'd; and Heav'n that hour let fall a tear;
Heav'n wept, that men might smile! Heav'n bled that men
Might never die!—
O'er guilt (how mountainous) with out-stretch'd arms,
Stern justice, and soft-smiling love, embrace,
Supporting, in full majesty, His throne,
When seem'd its majesty to need support,
Or that or man inevitably lost.
What but the fathomless of thought divine,
Could labour such expedient from despair,
And rescue both? both rescue! Both exalt !

O how are both exalted by the deed!
The wond'rous deed! or shall I call it more?
A wonder in omnipotence itself!
A mystery to angels, and to men!

The theme, the joy, what mortal can sustain?
See the burst gates! crush'd sting! demolish'd throne!
Last gasp of vanquish'd death! Shout, earth and heav'n
This sum of good to man.—Where roll my thoughts
To rest from wonders? other wonders rise;
And strike where'er they roll: my soul is caught:
Heaven's sovereign blessings, clust'ring from the cross,
Rush on her in a throng, and close her round,
The pris'ner of amaze!—In His blest Life,
I see the path, and in His death, the price,
And in His great ascent, the proof supreme,
Of immortality!

SECTION 2

HIS PERSON IS PRECIOUS.

His glory is so great as to surpass the comprehension of finite minds. But that degree of knowledge which a Christian has of His person by faith, is more valuable than any other kind of knowledge whatever. The apostle Paul, who knew how to estimate it, calls it "the excellency of the knowledge of Christ Jesus the Lord." He justly counted all things but loss in comparison with this, which shews how precious Christ was to him. Our future blessedness will consist in being with Him where He is, and beholding His glory.

The evangelist John, speaking of the person of Christ, tells us, "The word was made flesh, and dwelt among us." But what or whom does he mean by the word? "That Word which was in the beginning, which was with God, which was God, by whom all things were made, and without whom was not any thing made that was made." The Word was made flesh by the assumption of human nature, so as to be Immanuel, God with us. This was set forth in the divine prediction concerning His incarnation. "Unto us a child is born, unto us a Son is given, and the government shall be upon His shoulder; and His name shall be called Wonderful, Counsellor, The Mighty God, The Everlasting Father, The Prince of Peace."

Such is the dignity of Christ's person, that "he who hath seen Him, hath seen the Father also." He tells us in another place, that He is in the Father, and the Father in Him; that is, in the unity of the same Divine essence; for He and the Father are one.

He only who is over all, God blessed for ever, was able to execute the business of our salvation, which required the exertion of unbounded wisdom and almighty power.

But it was necessary, in order to the accomplishment of the great work of our redemption, that He should appear in our nature. For in His Divine nature, simply considered, He could not bear our sins, give His life a ransom for our souls, nor rise again for our justification. Neither was there that peculiar relation between His Divine nature and ours, which could give us a special interest in what was done by Him. Forasmuch therefore as the children were partakers of flesh and blood, He Himself likewise took part of the same. This alliance between Him and us was needful, to entitle us to the benefits of His meditation. It was thus, that He became our near kinsman, to whom belonged the right of redemption, and from whom alone we could claim relief in our ruined condition. On His becoming man, therefore our deliverance from misery and destruction absolutely depended.

He, in infinite compassion and condescension, sanctified a portion of our nature unto Himself, and took it to be His own, in a holy and mysterious subsistence in His own person. By so doing, He has exalted our nature above the whole creation. For the Father hath set the incarnate Saviour at His own right hand, in the heavenly places, far above all principalities, and powers, and might, and dominion, and every name that is named, not only in this world, but also in that which is to come. In this view, the Lord Jesus ought to be, and really is precious to them that believe. They see their own nature delivered from the lowest degree of debasement into which it was brought by sin, and most gloriously and divinely exalted in the person of their Redeemer. This consideration affords consolation and delight to their souls. He must surely be precious unto them, who has assumed their very nature into a substantial union with Himself, so that all the fulness of the God-head dwells bodily, substantially, and eternally in it. Never can we sufficiently admire the depths of Divine wisdom, condescension, and love displayed in this mystery of godliness.

In His incarnation, He becomes the representative image of God to us without whom our understandings cannot make any intimate approaches to the Divine nature. We behold the glory of the Deity in the face of Jesus Christ. With great propriety He is therefore said to be "The image of the invisible God; the brightness of His Father's glory, and the express image of His person."

The wonderful union of the divine and human natures in Christ, renders Him an object of admiration and adoration both to angels and men. "Without controversy great is the mystery of godliness; God was manifest in the flesh, justified in the Spirit, seen of angels, preached unto the Gentiles, believed on in the world, received up into glory." In the person of Christ we behold the most wonderful and astonishing display of Divine wisdom, grace and power. The whole mystery of godliness is resolved into this one article, that God was manifest in the flesh. This is the foundation on which alone faith can rest with security, and the distressed conscience find peace. The inspired apostle does not scruple to say, that "God hath purchased the church with His own blood." That is, He did so who was both God and man in one person. His blood may well be of sufficient efficacy to cleanse us from all sin, and to purge our consciences from dead works.

He is the sovereign Lord of all. The whole universe is under His government, and at His control. He doeth whatever He pleaseth in the armies of heaven, and among the inhabitants of the earth. The mightiest monarchs are but as worms beneath His feet. The thrones, principalities and powers of heaven are subject unto Him. He is "higher than the heavens," with all their shining hosts.

"Who," it is asked, "hath measured the waters in the hollow of His hand? Who hath meted out heaven with a span, and comprehended the dust of the earth in a measure, and weighed the mountains in scales, and the hills in a balance?" According to the representation of the enraptured prophet Isaiah, who saw His glory, and spake of Him, it is even He who shall feed His flock like a shepherd, who shall gather the lambs with His arm, and carry them in His bosom. "Behold the nations," continues he, "are as the drop of a bucket, and are counted as the small dust of the balance: behold He taketh up the isles, as a very little thing. All nations before Him are as nothing; and they are counted to Him as less than nothing and vanity."

His knowledge is without bounds or limits; for He knoweth all things. His wisdom is perfect; for He is the wisdom of God. His power is infinite; for He is the Almighty. His riches are immense. "To me who am less than the least of all saints is this grace given, that I should preach among the Gentiles the unsearchable riches of Christ."

Whatever benefit or blessing we stand in need of, His grace is sufficient, more than sufficient to bestow it. He is able to save sinners to the uttermost. Being one with the divine Father, He knows, He wills, He performs the same things as the Father doth. In His mediatorial capacity, He is the absolute Lord of life and death. He is the head over all things to the church, and manages all providences and all ordinances as He pleases, for the church's good. The book of life, and the keys of hell and death are in His hand. He executes His office with the greatest fidelity, for the honour of the Father, and the salvation of men. What a safe, what a suitable object of faith is Immanuel! There is all the ground that we can desire for the firmest confidence in Him, and reliance upon Him.

Being in the form of God, He thought it not robbery to be equal with God, He counted it no usurpation to claim a full equality of nature with the Father, since He and the Father are essentially one. Hence all men should honour the Son even as they honour the Father. To Him the following address is made, "Thy throne, O God, is for ever and ever." All the angels in heaven are commanded to worship Him, or to pay the same adoration to Him as to the Father. For there is no perfection attributed to the Father, but the same is attributed to the Son, in equal degree, and equal glory. As such, He is infinitely worthy of all possible esteem, love and service, both from men and angels. He claims equality with the Father in His Divine operations, "My Father worketh hitherto, and I work." His work and authority are the same with those of the Father, in the preservation and government of all things. And hence the apostle assures us, that "by Him, and through Him, and to Him are all things."

That the Divine Redeemer is man cannot be doubted by those who, with proper attention, read the history of His life upon earth. His hunger and thirst, His labours and sorrows, His stripes and wounds, His offering up strong cries and tears, His pains and His death, fully prove His real manhood. But when we contemplate Him in His transfiguration on the holy mount, we behold His glory, the glory as of the only-begotten of the Father, full of grace and truth. Then the Divinity, enshrined within His manhood, communicated its radiance outwardly to His body, and even to His garments. "His face did shine as the sun, and His raiment was white as the light." He was "clothed with majesty and honour; He decked Himself with light as with a garment."

When we contemplate the wonderful works which He performed, we see that He is the true God, and eternal life. The most boisterous elements in nature cease from raging, and compose themselves into a perfect calm, when he gives the powerful command, "Peace, be still." The most foul and inveterate leprosy is perfectly removed, and that in a moment, when He says, "Be thou clean." The body which had been four days in the state of the dead, returns to life, and rises from the tomb, when He says, "Lazarus, come forth." Disease and death, yea, the legions of darkness are obedient to His omnipotent word. Surely this is the Lord of nature; this is God manifest in the flesh. This is He who says of Himself, "I am Alpha and Omega, the First and the Last."

The nature which sinned, according to the rules of justice, was to suffer for sin. The Word, or the Son of God was therefore made flesh, that He might, as He said at His baptism, "fulfil all righteousness." He was incarnate, that He might have somewhat to offer, more valuable and efficacious than the flesh of bulls and of goats. "Sacrifice and offering Thou wouldest not, but a body hast Thou prepared me. In burnt offering and sacrifices for sin Thou hast had no pleasure; then said I, Lo I come, (in the volume of the book it is written of me,) to do Thy will, O God." And as Christ took manhood, that by it He might be capable of death, so, because manhood is the proper subject of compassion and sympathy, he, who without our nature could not suffer for the sins of men on earth, doth now, by means of that nature, make intercession for sinners, and exercise dominion over all men, with a true, a natural, and a sensible touch of pity.[23]

---

23 *Hooker's* Eccles. Polity. v. 51

I must beg leave to refer the reader to the learned Dr. Owen, and other able writers, who have given us at large the Scripture doctrine concerning the person of Christ. My present design is only to contemplate the subject in a cursory and devotional way. I freely own, that I am lost when I meditate on the glory of Immanuel. He formed the heavens by His word, and all the host of them by the breath of His mouth. He filleth the whole universe with His immensity. My faith ascends to Him in the palace of His glory, surrounded with thousands of thousands, and ten thousand times ten thousand mighty angels, always ready to execute His will. And did He become incarnate for us men, and for our salvation? I look down upon myself and say, What am I? Lord, what is man, that Thou shouldst be thus mindful of him, and the son of man that Thou shouldst so regard him? I am but an atom, I am but dust and ashes, and all overspread, with pollution and deformity. And can this atom, this dust, this deformed mass of impurity be the object of redeeming mercy? What motive could determine the Lord of glory to become man for my sake, and to communicate Himself in a manner so intimate, so endearing, to a creature so mean and vile? The seraphim round His throne cover their faces with their wings, and cry one to another, "Holy, holy, holy is the Lord of Hosts! The whole earth is full of His glory." Struck with a sense of His majesty, how justly may I exclaim with the prophet, "Woe is me! I am a man of unclean lips." May one of the seraphs come and touch my lips, with a live coal from His altar!

There is an incomparable and transcendent excellency in the person of Christ, in every respect. He is fairer than the children of men; He is altogether lovely. The excellencies which are found in any of His creatures are as nothing, when compared with His excellency. Wisdom in them is but a beam; but He is the glorious Sun of Righteousness. Goodness in them is but as the drop of a bucket; but He is the fountain, the ocean of goodness. Holiness in them is but a glimmering spark, but He is the brightness of His Father's glory, and the express image of His person. He is equal in all glorious excellencies with the Father. His divine nature puts infinite dignity on His amazing condescension, gives eternal efficacy to the sacrifice which He offered up to expiate our sins, and to the righteousness He wrought out to justify our persons.

The righteousness of a mere creature, however highly exalted, could not have been accepted by the Sovereign of the universe, as any compensation for our disobedience. For whoever undertakes to bear the penalty of the law, and fulfil its precepts in the room of others, must be one who is not obliged to obedience on His own account. Consequently, our surety must be a divine person; for every mere creature is under indispensable obligations to perfect and perpetual obedience. And, as our situation required, so the gospel reveals, a Mediator and substitute thus exalted and glorious. For He is described as one who could, without arrogance, or the least disloyalty, claim independence; claim full equality with the Father. Hence it was by His own voluntary condescension that He became incarnate, and took upon Him the form of a servant. And, by the same free act of His will, He was made under the law, to perform that obedience in our stead, to which, as a divine person, He was in no sense obliged.

The nature of our Redeemer's work, as Mediator, made it necessary that He should be both God and man in one person. Deity alone was too high to treat with man; humanity alone was too low to treat with God. The eternal Son, therefore, assumed our nature, that He might become a middleperson, a Mediator between God and men, capable of "laying His hands upon both," and of bringing sinful man and his offended Maker into a state of perfect friendship. He could not, in office, have been a Mediator, if He had not, in His natures, been a middle-person.[24]

---

24 See *Booth's* Reign of Grace, Chap. xi

The constitution of the Redeemer's person is the effect of infinite wisdom, almighty power, and unbounded love. It is here that the foundation is laid for our hope of everlasting happiness. There is enough in this subject to excite astonishment, gratitude and joy through eternal ages. It is not sufficient to say that it is mysterious; it is mystery itself; the mystery of godliness; the wisdom of God is a mystery. Yet the truth and certainty of it are clearly revealed; and though it be a stone of stumbling, and a rock of offence to them who stumble at the word, being disobedient; yet to those that believe, it is, and for ever will be, precious!

Though the proof of our doctrine concerning the person of Christ is derived from the sacred Scriptures, yet the testimony of the first Christian writers is not to be despised, because it shews what their sentiments were who lived nearest the apostle's days, and how they understood the sacred oracles. For the sake of brevity, I shall only refer to one.

Justin Martyr, whom we have mentioned before, flourished in the second century. He was a native of Neapolis, a noted city of Palestine, in the province of Samaria, anciently called Sichem. He was a Grecian by birth and religion. In his Gentile state he was bewildered in the mazes of the vain philosophy which was then taught, and after many searches and re-searches concerning God and happiness, full of darkness, full of anxiety, and as a benighted traveler, not knowing which way to take, it pleased the Almighty at length to lead him into the path of truth and peace. He met with a simple, plain old man, who directed him to the sacred Scriptures. In examining these divine writings, his mind was illuminated, his wounded conscience was relieved by the discovery of that remedy which God has provided for the recovery of ruined man, and he found rest to his soul.

Having found the pearl of great price, he went, to use the words of our Divine Redeemer, and sold all that he had, and bought it.

All the vain treasures he had amassed together, from the writings of the Pythagoreans, Peripatetics, Stoics, and even from those of his beloved Plato, he freely renounced, as useless encumbrances to his mind, and embraced that precious gospel, that doctrine of Christ crucified, which was to the Jews a stumblingblock, and to the Greeks foolishness. He did this at the certain expense of every worldly comfort, and even of life itself; for he suffered martyrdom, and that with holy boldness and resignation, in defence of the truth which he had so heartily espoused.

Justin was at Rome, when the persecution against the Christians broke out afresh, under the reign of the emperor Antoninus Pius. Here he wrote his *Apologies for the Christians*, the first at least, if not the second. I am far from undertaking to vindicate every thing contained in these books, which are valuable cheifly for their antiquity, and for the account they give us of the faith and practise of Christians at this early period. The design of them is to lay before the emperor, the senate, and the people, the injustice of their proceedings against the followers of Christ. He observes, that they were hunted after with all the art and diligence which malice could invent, and when discovered, inhumanly dragged to the tribunal, where, against all known rules of equity, they were condemned, not for any crime, but simply on account of their religion. If a man did but own himself a Christian, he was, without farther trial, doomed to the worst of deaths.

In matters of doctrine, this writer sometimes indulged his fancy too far, and endeavoured to explain, by philosophical reasonings, those mysterious truths which do not admit of any efforts of that kind, but ought to be received with humble simplicity, on the authority of him who has revealed them. But such passages as the following are very valuable, and deserving of peculiar notice.

"There were of old among the Jews, certain prophets of God, by whom the prophetic spirit made proclamation of things to come, long before they were in being. These prophecies, just as they were delivered, were committed to writing by the prophets themselves, in their own Hebrew mothertongue, and the books put into the custody of the kings of Judea.

"Now, in these books of the prophets, we find it foretold, that there was one to come into the world, who being born of a virgin, and grown up to man's estate, should cure every disease and malady in nature, and raise the dead; that this Jesus our Christ, should be treated with spite and ignominy; should be fastened to a cross and die; that He should rise again and ascend up to heaven; that He being truly the Son of God, should be worshipped under that title; that He should send out some to preach these tidings to every nation; and that the Gentiles should be brought to believe in His name, in greater numbers than the Jews.

"Moses, the prince of prophets, thus expressly signified, 'The sceptre shall not depart from Judah, nor a law-giver from between His feet, until Shiloh come, and unto Him shall the gathering of the people be; binding His foal unto the vine, and washing His garments in the blood of grapes." It is incumbent on you (Romans) to make diligent inquiry, how long the Jews had a prince or ruler properly their own; and you will find that, after the coming of Shiloh, or Jesus Christ, our Master, you yourselves reigned over the Jews, and reduced their whole kingdom into a Roman province.'

"The 'binding His foal unto the vine, and washing His garments in the blood of grapes,' was a significant symbol of what Christ was to do and suffer; for there stood the foal of an ass tied to a vine, at the entrance of a certain village, which He ordered His disciples to go and bring Him; upon this beast He rode into Jerusalem, where the stately temple of the Jews then was, which you since have rased to the ground. To fulfil the sequel of the prophecy, He was afterwards crucified. For 'washing His garments in the blood of grapes,' prefigured the passion He was to undergo, purifying by His blood such as should believe in Him. For by what the Divine Spirit calls His garments are signified the faithful, in whom the Logos, the Word of God dwells.

"Isaiah, another prophet, foretels the same things, but in other words; 'There shall come a star out of Jacob, and a rod shall come forth out of the root of Jesse, and to it shall the Gentiles seek.' This shining star out of Jacob, this rod out of the root of Jesse, is Christ; who was conceived by the power of God, and born of a virgin, of the seed of Jacob; and Jesse, according to this oracle, was reckoned among His ancestors; but He was the son of Jacob and Judah in a lineal succession. Concerning Christ's being born of a virgin, hear the express words of the same prophet; 'Behold, a virgin shall conceive, and bear a Son, and shall call His name Immanuel, that is, God with us.' Such things as were, in the opinions of men, incredible. God, by the prophetic Spirit, foretold that which should come to pass. The mother of Jesus conceived in the pure state of virginity. The angel of God, which was sent to her, delivered his message in these words; 'Behold thou shalt conceive in thy womb by the Holy Ghost, and bring forth a Son; and He shall be called the Son of the Highest; and thou shalt call His name Jesus, for He shall save His people from their sins.' So the evangelists, whom we believe, have taught us.

"David, another prophet, says, 'They pierced My hands and My feet, and upon My vesture did they cast lots.' David, who spake this, suffered nothing like it. But the hands of Jesus Christ were pierced, and extended upon a cross, while the Jews reviled Him, and denied Him to be the Messiah. When they had crucified Him, they parted His garments, and cast lots upon His vesture; for the truth of which you may satisfy yourselves from the acts of Pontius Pilate."

After the citation of many other prophecies concerning Jesus Christ, the apologist adds, "What motive could ever possibly have persuaded us to believe a crucified man to be the first begotten of the eternal God, and that He should come be the Judge of all the world, had we not met with those prophetic testimonies of Him, proclaimed so long before His incarnation? Were we not eye-witnesses to the fulfilling of them? Did we not see the desolation of Judea, and men out of all nations proselyted to the faith by His apostles, renouncing the ancient errors in which they were brought up? Did we not find the prophecies made good in ourselves, and see Christians in greater number, and of greater sincerity from among the Gentiles, than from among the Jews and Samaritans?"

It may be observed in general, that though this writer appears to be somewhat bewildered and obscure, especially when he attempts to explain to the heathens the sonship of Christ, yet he bears his testimony to the dignity of his person again and again. Thus when he quotes that passage. "No man knoweth the Son but the Father, neither knoweth any man the Father save the Son, and he to whomsoever the Son will reveal Him," he adds, "Christ Himself accused the unbelieving Jesus of being ignorant concerning both the Father and the Son; for they who affirm the Son to be the Father, know not the Father, neither do they know the Son, who being the Logos, and first-begotten of God, is also God."

He addresses the emperor and the senate with great boldness, and says, "I could wish you to take this into serious consideration, that what we say is for your own good. For it is in our power at any time, to escape your torments, by denying the faith when you question us about it; but we scorn to purchase life at the expense of a lie. For our souls are winged with desire of a life of eternal duration and purity, of an immediate converse with God, the Maker of all things. We long to finish our course of faith, being fully persuaded that we shall arrive at that blissful state. When you hear us express our expectation of a kingdom, you rashly conclude, it must be a kingdom on earth, notwithstanding all we can say to the contrary. We profess ourselves Christians upon examination, when we know death to be the certain consequence of such a profession. But were our thoughts fixed upon a kingdom in this world, we should surely deny our religion for the preservation of our lives, and have recourse to all the methods of concealment, in order that we might enjoy the object of our wishes. But since our hopes do not fix on things present, the preservation of our lives is not so weighty a concern with us. We know that all must die, and our murderers can but cut us short a few days, of what might rationally be expected to be the period of our existence here."

He concludes thus; "So far as these things shall appear agreeable to truth and reason, so far we desire you to regard them; if they seem trifling, regard them as trifles. However, do not proceed against the professors of them, who are a people of the most inoffensive lives, as severely as you would against your professed enemies. For I must tell you, that if you persist in this course of iniquity, you cannot escape the vengeance of God in the other world. But be that as it may, you shall hear us contentedly cry out, *The will of God be done!*"[25]

SECTION 3

HIS NAMES ARE PRECIOUS.

The very sound of His name gladdens the hearts of them that believe. He is called by a variety of names, to set forth that variety of excellencies which meet in Him. The prophet gives us a pleasing catalogue of some of those in one verse: "For unto us a child is born, unto us a Son is given, and the government shall be upon His shoulder; and His name shall be called, Wonderful, Counsel-

---

25 *Justin Mart.* ubi. supra. lxxxiv, &c. apud *Grabem.*

lor, The mighty God, The everlasting Father, The Prince of Peace."
Every one of these names is instructive, significant, and expressive
of what He is in Himself, and what He is to us, wretched sinners,
who are enriched by His benefits. They may well therefore be precious to us. They administer peace to the distracted bosom, healing
to the broken heart, and consolation to the desponding mind.

Some have been at the pains to reckon up above one hundred
and fifty different names, by which the divine Saviour is called
in the Old and New Testaments. It may suffice us to single out a
few of these. In that divine pastoral, the Song of Solomon, where
many of the amiable appearances in nature are employed to set
forth His love, the excellency of His person, and the happiness
of those who have communion with Him, we have the following beautiful passage, "Thy name is as ointment poured forth,
therefore do the virgins love thee."[26] As ointment and perfume

---

26   I am fully persuaded, in my own mind, that the *Song of* Solomon is a part of
      that Scripture which was given by the inspiration of God. There never was any
      controversy about its authenticity among the *Jews*, to whom were committed the
      oracles of God. They say in their *Misnah, All the Scriptures are holy, but the Song of
      Songs is the holy of holies*. Christians of all ages, a few only excepted, have always
      esteemed it sacred and venerable. Ancient councils included it in their catalogues of
      the canonical books of Scripture, and some of the first Christian writers published
      comments upon it, as *Eusebius* informs us.

      It agrees with other parts of the sacred writings. The forty-fifth psalm, which was
      written by *David*, Solomon's father, is exactly in the same strain with this Song,
      and bears a striking resemblance of it, both as to its subject, and its style or manner.
      In many of our Lord's discourses, as recorded by the Evangelists, there are manifest
      allusions to this book. A few instances shall suffice: Draw me, we will run after thee;
      No man can come to me except the Father draw him; Awake, O north wind, and
      come thou south, and blow upon my garden; The wind bloweth where it listeth;
      Pleasant fruits, new and old, which I have laid up for thee; Bring forth out of his
      treasure things new and old; He let out the vineyard unto keepers; He planted a
      vineyard, and let it out to husbandmen; I sleep, but my heart waketh; The ten
      virgins all slumbered and slept. So when our Lord calls Himself the Bridegroom,
      and His disciples the children of the bride-chamber, He adopts the same figures
      which are used throughout that book.

      That *John*, in his book of Revelation, refers to the Song of *Solomon*, seems
      undeniable, when he speaks of the marriage of the Lamb, of the Lamb's wife,
      and of the joyful solemnity of the marriage-supper. The glorious person of Christ

rejoice the heart, so those titles given to our Redeemer, which are peculiarly expressive of His work, His grace, or His glory, afford pleasure and edification to those who are desirous of giving their choicest affections to Him.

1. The name Jesus, which signifies a Saviour, and was given to Him because He saves His people from their sins, is a name very dear to those that believe. They have seen the exceeding sinfulness of sin, and beheld themselves in a perishing condition because of it; as such the news of a Saviour is to them as life from the dead. That intelligence of His name and salvation, which the gospel brings to their ears, is like the breaking and pouring forth of a box of precious ointment, removing that sadness and sorrow of heart, which are occasioned by a sight and sense of their own sin and misery.

Bishop Pearson seems to have set the etymology of the name Jesus in the clearest light, by observing that JAH, one of the incommunicable names or God, enters into the composition of the Hebrew name Jehoshuah, to which Jesus answers.[27] This deriva-

---

is represented by both writers by figures which have a near resemblance to one another. John describes the drowsy state of the church, and Christ standing at the door and knocking, just as *Solomon* had done before Him. The two books in question are both concluded in the same manner. Make haste, my Beloved. Behold, I come quickly: Amen, even so come, Lord Jesus.

I hope the reader will excuse me, if I add a short note from Dr. *Owen*: speaking of communion with Christ, he says, "As this is intimated in many places of Scripture, so there is one entire book designed to set it forth. This is *divine Song of Solomon*, who was a type of Christ, and a penman of the Holy Ghost therein. It is a gracious record of the divine communications of Christ in love and grace unto His church, with her returns of love to Him, and delight in Him. And then may a man judge himself to have somewhat profited, in the experience of the mystery of a blessed intercourse and communion with Christ, when the expressions of them, in that holy dialogue, give light and life to his mind, and efficaciously communicate unto him an experience of their power. But because these things are little *understood* by many, the *book* itself is much neglected, if not despised. Yea, to such impudence have some arrived, in foaming out their own shame, as that they have ridiculed the expressions of it; but we are foretold of such *mockers* in the last days, who should walk after their own *ungodly lusts*; they are not of our present consideration."— *Glory of Christ*, page 105.

27   *Pearson* on the Creed, page 69–71.

tion most plainly shews, how Christ's being called Jesus was, as the sacred historian suggests, in effect, an accomplishment of the prophecy, that He should be called Immanuel. "Thou shalt call His name Jesus. This was done that it might be fulfilled which was spoken of the Lord by the prophet, saying, They shall call His name Immanuel, which being interpreted, is, God with us." It is intimated here, that the name Jesus is, in signification, equivalent to that of Immanuel, or God in our nature. He must be man as well as God, and God as well as man; otherwise He could not be the Saviour of ruined sinners. But being both in one person, He was capable of suffering what was necessary to be suffered, and of performing what was needful to be performed, in order to accomplish the great design.

The reason given by the heavenly messenger, why He must be called Jesus, serves to set forth the signification of the name, "For He shall save His people from their sins." To save them is, on the one hand, to rescue them from evils which it is not in the power of language to describe; and, on the other, to confer upon them an infinite good.

Some of the grandest titles of the almighty are joined in the Old Testament, with this term Saviour. "I, even I, am Jehovah, and besides Me there is no Saviour. I am Jehovah, there is no God else besides me; a just God, and a Saviour; there is none besides Me. I am the Lord thy God, the holy one of Israel, thy Saviour. All flesh shall know that I the Lord am thy Saviour, and thy Redeemer, the Mighty One of Jacob. O the Hope of Israel, the Saviour thereof!" Of such a Saviour we wretched sinners stood in need, and such a Saviour Jesus is, as appears from the united testimony of the inspired writers.

How full of comfort then must this precious name be, to every believing soul! Jesus, the Saviour, God with us, the Son of God in our nature, full of tenderness, unbounded love, almighty in power, able to offer up a sacrifice for our sins of infinite value, able to conquer all enemies, to overcome all opposition, to bestow every saving blessing upon us, and to fulfil in us all the good pleasure of His goodness and the work of faith with power. The blessedness derived from Him is immense and everlasting. All that is experienced of it in this world is but an earnest of what is reserved for that which is to come. Well may every Christian say, "My soul doth magnify the Lord, and my spirit hath rejoiced in God my Saviour! He has a name above every name, that at the name of Jesus every knee should bow, and that every tongue should confess that Jesus Christ is Lord, to the glory of God the Father."

> *Jesus! I love Thy charming name,*
> *'Tis music to mine ear;*
> *Fain would I sound it out so loud*
> *That earth and heaven should hear.*
>
> *Yes, Thou art precious to my soul,*
> *My transport and my trust:*
> *Jewels to Thee are gaudy toys,*
> *And gold is sordid dust.*
>
> *All my capacious powers can wish,*
> *In Thee doth richly meet;*
> *Not to mine eyes is light so dear,*
> *Nor friendship half so sweet.*
>
> *Thy name still dwells upon my heart,*
> *And sheds its fragrance there:*
> *The noblest balm of all its wounds,*
> *The cordial of its care.*
>
> *I'll speak the honours of Thy name*
> *With my expiring breath;*
> *Then speechless clasp Thee in my arms,*
> *And thus be blest in death.*

2. He is called Messiah, and in that character is also precious to believers. With a lively faith they behold in Him the exact accomplishment of the various prophecies of the Old Testament concerning the Redeemer of mankind. The seed of Abraham, and of David; born of a virgin, poor and obscure, and yet one whom David called his Lord; a great king, an everlasting priest, though not of the tribe of Levi; born at Bethlehem; a prophet like unto Moses, but greater than he. They behold Him as one who would preach good tidings to the meek and the poor; as one who should proclaim liberty to the captives, should comfort the mourners, and heal the broken in heart; who should publish His gospel first in the land of Zebulon and Naphtali, in Galilee of the Gentiles, and then throughout the coasts of Israel; who should have a forerunner in the spirit and with the power of Elijah, crying in the wilderness, "Prepare ye the way of the Lord, make His paths straight."

They see from the prophets, that the Messiah was to be one who should come unto the daughter of Zion, meek, lowly, and riding upon an ass's colt; who should work miracles more than Moses and all the ancient prophets, miracles of a mild, merciful, and beneficent kind; who should open the eyes of the blind, unstop the ears of the deaf, make the tongue of the dumb to sing, and the lame man to leaps as an hart.

They perceive that the Messiah was to be one, who, notwithstanding all the displays of His power and goodness, should be rejected by the greater part of the Jews, to whom He should be a stumblingblock, and a rock of offence. They see that He was to be one who should be despised and afflicted, a man of sorrows, and cut off from the land of the living; who should have numerous enemies, that would hate Him without a cause. They see that He was to be accused by false witnesses, betrayed by a pretended friend, sold for thirty pieces of silver, which money should be given for a potter's field, after it had been thrown away by the perfidious traitor, who should come to a miserable end.

They see that the enemies of the Messiah should use Him in a very barbarous and shameful manner; that they should buffet Him, and spit in His face; that He should be led like a lamb to the slaughter, not opening His mouth, save only to intercede for these transgressors; they should strip Him of His raiment, dividing it among themselves by lot; they should surround Him like furious bulls, pierce His hands and His feet, mock Him in the midst of His agonies, shaking their heads at Him, and giving Him gall and vinegar to drink; that He should be reduced to such a state by His sufferings, that His heart should melt within Him like wax, His bones be dislocated, and His tongue cleave to the roof of His mouth; that His hands and His feet should be pierced, and yet not one of His bones broken; that in His expiring agonies He should cry, "My God, My God, why hast Thou forsaken Me?" They see that He should be numbered with transgressors, and after He had been put to a shameful death, be laid in the sepulchre of a rich man, whence He should rise again the third day, before He had seen corruption; that he should ascend up to heaven, sit at the right hand of the Father, be crowned with glory and honour, see His seed, the happy fruits of the travail of His soul, and be satisfied.[28]

While all these, and many other prophecies are found to have their exact accomplishment in Jesus Christ, even as face answereth to face in a glass, He certainly ought to be endeared to our hearts. We should say with the enraptured Nathaniel, that Israelite indeed, "We have found the Messiah, of whom Moses in the law, and the prophets did write, even Jesus of Nazareth; He is indeed the very Christ, the anointed of God, and the Author of eternal salvation.

---

28   See *Dr. Jortin's* Remarks on Eccles. History, vol. i, page 112.

3. He is called, The Prince of Peace.

Sin had put an end to all friendly intercourse between man and his Maker, but Jesus undertook to make up the breach. Let others dream of reconciliation with God, on the ground of absolute mercy, without satisfaction for sin; I can form no idea of such a reconciliation, as there is a total silence about it in the Scriptures of truth. Thy mercy, O my God, is never exercised to the prejudice of Thy awful justice. The severity of Thy justice is not lost in the freeness of Thy mercy, nor the freeness of Thy mercy in the strictness of Thy justice. It is daring insolence in any sinful creature, to imagine he can have peace with Thee in a way dishonourable to truth and righteousness.

"We have violated that holy law, by which Thou dost govern the world. The penalty must fall on the delinquent, if an interposing Mediator does not make up the breach. But Thy own eternal Son, in order to make peace, has brought a price in His hand, a price adequate to the wrong done to Thee, O my God, and to the offence committed against Thee. A price, which was sufficient to stop the course of Thy awful justice, sufficient to accomplish the wonderful design, that Thou mightest be abundantly satisfied, and well pleased with those who once were enemies. Thy wrath is laid aside; he that was a rebel and a traitor, being once subdued, is received into the bosom of Thy favour, and enjoys that friendship with God, which shall abide for ever. The virtue of my Redeemer's sacrifice is such that it reaches back to the first Adam, and forward to the end of the world, and will be as efficacious then as it was the first moment it was offered.

"Blessed Jesus, Prince of Peace, there is none but Thyself to screen my guilty soul from Divine displeasure. How precious art Thou to me, when I consider, what a fearful thing it is to fall into the hands of the living God! Who can dwell with devouring fire? Who can endure everlasting burnings? Yet these must have been my portion, if Thou hadst not espoused my cause. And these will be the portion of all those who reject Thy mediation. Were there any other expedient, somewhat might be said to excuse their folly. But this is the last, the sovereign, the only remedy.

"And may this remedy be ever dear to my heart! Dearer than the light which salutes my eyes; dearer than the food which supports my life; yea, dearer than life itself. To Thee, blessed Saviour, my everlasting thanks are due, for Thy kind interposition in my favour, to make peace by the blood of the cross. Without this, I could never have had access to the Father; I could never have enjoyed communion with God here, nor the pleasing hope of being admitted into His presence hereafter. But a new and living way is now opened. Through the Prince of Peace, I have boldness and access with confidence. And the blessing of reconciliation is permanent as well as great. Jesus everlastingly maintains that peace which He hath once procured. It is a lasting blessing, since He hath obtained eternal redemption for us."

4. He is called "The Lord of glory." So the apostle Paul, in his former epistle to the Corinthians, speaks of Him: "Which none of the princes of this world knew; for had they known Him, they would not have crucified the Lord of glory." His person is glorious. His works are glorious. The liberty He grants to those who had been the captives of sin and Satan, is a glorious liberty. The gospel which reveals Him is a glorious gospel. The church His mystical body, is a glorious church; such indeed it will be, when He presents it to Himself, without spot or wrinkle, or any such thing. His kingdom is a glorious kingdom, and His throne is the throne of glory.

His essential glory, as God, and one with the Father, is not only unspeakable, but inconceivable. His honour, His name, His essential properties and perfections, His nature, and His will are the same with those of the Father. Of this He assures us, when He says, "All things that the Father hath are mine."

The glory which belongs to Him as Mediator, and head of the church, is exceedingly great. Of this the apostle speaks, when he tells us, that "God hath highly exalted Him, and given Him a name which is above every name; that at the name of Jesus every knee should bow, of things in heaven, and things in earth, and things under the earth; and that every tongue should confess that Jesus Christ is Lord, to the glory of God the Father."

As He is the Lord of glory, He has that at His disposal, and will bestow it on His followers. Thus when addressing His divine Father, He said, "The glory which Thou gavest Me, I have given them." He will therefore appoint unto them a kingdom, as the Father hath appointed unto Him. They know that when He shall appear, they must also appear with Him in glory. Their souls shall be filled and adorned with glory, and even their vile bodies shall be fashioned like unto His glorious body, according to the working whereby He is able to subdue all things unto Himself.

His name, as the Lord of glory, is precious to them that believe. They desire to have daily more and more acquaintance with Him, and to grow in the sweet and powerful experience of that intercourse which is carried on between a glorious Redeemer in heaven, and His saints on earth. Let us suppose the true Christian, in His retired moments, addressing God in such manner as the following:

"Thou O God art unchangeable in Thy nature, glorious in Thine essence, wonderful in Thy perfections, wise in Thy counsels, and holy in all Thy works. It is my greatest good and highest happiness to enjoy Thy favour, and to behold the glory of Thy countenance. Permit me to say, with Thy servant *Moses*, 'I beseech Thee, shew me Thy glory.' I only request such a view of it in this world, as it is proper for a mortal creature, in the midst of the frailty and imperfection which are inseparable from the present state. Shew me the glory of Thy wisdom, Thy holiness, Thy power, Thy grace, and thy mercy in Christ Jesus. This will give me a distaste for the gaudy vanities of the present world. I shall then look with indifference on all that after which the covetous are eagerly panting. I shall pity the ambitious, in their restless solicitude to make themselves great, and to obtain the veneration of their fellow-creatures, whose breath is in their nostrils. Thy Divine beauty and infinite loveliness, as displayed in the glorious Mediator, will captivate my desires, inflame my love, and excite my joy and delight.

"A more intimate view of Thy holiness will imbitter every sin, and lead me, in deepest humiliation, to abhor myself, and repent as in dust and ashes. Give me such a sense of Thy majesty, as may dispose my heart to reverence Thee supremely. Afford me such discoveries of Thy omnipotence, Thy love, and Thy goodness, as may support my fainting heart under the toils of this warfare, and all the afflictions attending the state of mortality; that I may endure them all as 'seeing Him who is invisible.' Let the impressions which Thy adorable perfections make upon me be deep and powerful, so as to transform my soul into Thy own amiable and holy likeness. Thus by beholding the glory of the Lord, may I be changed into the same image, from glory to glory, even as by the Spirit of the Lord.

"It is habitual, and not transient communion with Jesus, the Lord of glory, that will satisfy my desires, and produce those happy effects which I seek, of nearer conformity to Him, in knowledge, righteousness and true holiness. Let me hold daily converse with Him, and intensely contemplate His glory. If communion with wise men be the way to advance in wisdom, how much more will communion with Christ promote that noble end! How must it tend to refine the understanding, rectify the soul, and purify the heart! Grant me, O Thou Author of all good, by frequent converse with thee, to have my affections spiritualized, that I may look with indifference on all other objects, and have my conversation in heaven. In fellowship with Thee I shall find a source of delights, infinitely superior to any thing this world can afford. For Thy lovingkindness is better than life itself. Thou art the inexhaustible treasury of uncreated blessedness. O Lord God of hosts, blessed is the man that trusteth in Thee!"

5. He is called Strength. "The Lord Jehovah is my Strength, and my Song; He also is become my Salvation." It is He that giveth strength and power to His people. In Him they have not only righteousness, but strength. He is precious to the believer under this consideration, who is emboldened to say, with the apostle Paul, "I can do all things through Christ, who strengtheneth me."

God has formed all His works, both in nature and grace, so as perpetually to need His supporting hand. By so doing, He has laid us under a happy necessity of being dependent on Him. I am weak and therefore must be a dependent creature. I have to strive against numerous enemies, stronger than myself, and cannot stand my ground without strength from above. When a city is conquered by a mighty prince, some yield to the victor, and espouse his cause; but others will be forming designs to cast off the yoke. There is a necessity for the same power to keep it, as was at first exerted in subduing it. Such is the state of my soul. It relieves me to think, that my precious Saviour knows my need, and has promised to give strength according to the day. Strengthen, O Lord, that which Thou hast wrought!

"I would humble myself under a consciousness of my own unspeakable weakness, and would ever be sensible, that danger is nigh; but I would at the same time, rejoice in the happy necessity I am under of being constantly dependent on Him, who is mighty to save.

"Lord, Thou hast taught me, by daily experience, that I stand in need of Thy supporting power on all occasions. May Thy everlasting arm be underneath me, and Thy strength be made perfect in my weakness. Renouncing all confidence in the flesh, may I, by a lively faith, be strong in the grace which is in Thee.

"I am not sufficient of myself even to think any thing properly and spiritually, much less am I able to perform any holy purpose, in a right and acceptable manner. It is the Lord who giveth strength both to will and to do of His good pleasure. Having formed the soul for heavenly motion, and regulated the springs of action, His presence and agency are still continually necessary to bring it forward in the way of holiness. He is the author, the promoter, and the finisher of all good. When to will is present with me, yet how to perform that which is good I find not, but as Christ strengtheneth me. If I attempt to engage in any spiritual exercise, I no longer keep close to it than His Almighty hand upholds me, and leads me on. If I pray, I know not what to pray for as I ought, unless His Spirit help my infirmity. If I would hear the word, I need the same divine hand to open my heart, that I may profit by what I hear. In the whole of my Christian course, I find the words of my precious Redeemer verified, 'Without Me, (or separate from me) ye can do nothing.' "

6. He is called, "The Consolation of Israel." Simeon waited for the consolation of Israel. He is not only a comforter but comfort itself. Other comforts, when compared with Him, scarcely deserve the name. True believers rejoice in Christ Jesus, and have no confidence in the flesh. A command is given them to rejoice in Him always. The gospel which reveals Him is a joyful sound, the tidings it brings are glad tidings.

Jesus may well be called the Consolation of His people, as He saves them from everlasting misery, relieves them under present troubles, and advances them to the regions of eternal joy and felicity. All the consolation they have in this world is derived from Him. If they joy in God, it is through Jesus Christ our Lord, by whom they have now received the atonement. If they glory, it is in His cross. If they are of good cheer, it is because He has forgiven their sins. If they rejoice in hope of the glory of God, it is because Christ is in them, the hope of glory.

Hence we hear them that believe, expressing themselves in such language as this, "My soul doth magnify the Lord, and my spirit hath rejoiced in God my Saviour. I will greatly rejoice in the Lord, my soul shall be joyful in my God; for He hath clothed me with the garments of salvation, He hath covered me with the robe of righteousness, as a bridegroom decketh himself with ornaments, and as a bride adorneth herself with jewels."

Christ is to His people every thing they can need, every thing they can enjoy. Happy they who can claim interest with Him who is all and in all to them that love Him. If they renounce the pleasures of sin, they have joys infinitely beyond them.

Reader, you, like the rest of your fellow-creatures, are in quest of happiness; but, permit me to ask, Where do you seek it? Do you seek it in the wealth of this world? That is but a splendid encumbrance. Do you seek it in the honour which cometh from men? That is but a puff of noisy breath, a glittering bubble, which breaks almost as soon as it is formed. Do you seek happiness in the pleasures of sin? They are but for a season; they leave a sting behind, and end in misery and torment. Nay, even while you are in pursuit of them, you will find, that, like the briny waters of the ocean to a thirsty palate, they irritate rather than satisfy. Do you seek to get rid of disquieting thoughts in gay and jovial company? Alas! this is only a temporary opiate, not a lasting cure. And it is well, if, like an opiate when its power is spent, it does not leave the spirits disordered, flattened and sunk.

Learn to look for peace and happiness in Him who is the Consolation of Israel; in the discoveries of His boundless love, the precious promises of His gospel, and the hope of complete salvation and everlasting glory through Him. Here the true health, ease, and felicity of our nature are to be found.

SECTION 4

HIS OFFICES AND CHARACTERS ARE PRECIOUS.

The evangelist John tells us, that when Christ was upon earth, he and others "saw His glory, the glory as of the only-begotten of the Father, full of grace and truth." He cannot be understood to speak here of the glory of His outward condition; for Christ made Himself, in this respect, of no reputation, taking on Him the form of a servant. Nor is this to be interpreted directly and absolutely of the eternal, essential glory of His divine nature; for this cannot be seen in the present state. But the evangelist rather speaks of His glory as Mediator; for it is in the administration of that office that He is "full of grace and truth." This indeed implies His divine nature, as "the only-begotten of the Father." This glory of the Redeemer was seen, not with bodily eyes, but by faith; for John immediately afterwards tells us, that what he speaks of was the privilege only of those that *received Him, and believed on His name.*

God gave to His church, under the Old Testament, kings, priests, and prophets. He anointed them to their several offices, gave them directions as to the discharge of those offices, was present with them in their work, and accepted their services. These offices are all united in the person of our Lord Jesus Christ.

1. He is a Priest for ever after the order of Melchizedek. His priesthood was foretold in the writings of the prophets, and it is particularly insisted on by the apostles. The priestly office consists

of two branches, the offering of sacrifice, and making intercession. The sacrifice which Jesus had to offer was His life, which He
gave as a ransom for many. He offered Himself without spot to
God; and on this account, He is called the Lamb of God, which
taketh away the sin of the world. For the same reason He is said
to be set forth as a propitiation. Both the parts of His sacerdotal
office are mentioned by the apostle John, and their mutual relation to each other is hinted at, in the following words, "We have
an Advocate with the Father, Jesus Christ the righteous, and He
is the propitiation for our sins." His intercession with the Father,
as our Advocate, is grounded on His being a propitiation for our
sins. But we are indebted to the apostle to the Hebrews, for the
largest and clearest account of Christ's priesthood. Jesus may well
be precious in this capacity to those that believe, for His priesthood is the principal foundation of the faith and comfort of the
church. The subject is interesting and important in the highest
degree; but instead of a farther discussion of it in this place, I shall
only add the following aspiration:

"O Thou great and glorious High Priest, who art higher than
the heavens; Thou didst condescend to dwell with men upon
earth, and didst offer up Thyself an offering and a sacrifice of a
sweet-smelling savour. By that one offering Thou hast perfected
for ever them that are sanctified. Our sins stood between God
and us, like a dreadful wall of separation, but by Thy glorious
and all-sufficient atonement Thou hast effectually removed the
obstruction, and made the way of access to God and happiness
free and open, that the offended Majesty of heaven, and offending mortals when brought to repentance, might be united in the
bond of perpetual love. When sojourning here upon earth, Thou
didst call sinners, by Thy own voice, to partake of this privilege:
and Thou callest them still by the ministers of reconciliation, and
by Thy blessed word and gospel. Thou didst say to the trembling

sinner, "Be of good cheer, thy sins are forgiven thee." Let me also hear Thy pardoning voice; let me know, by happy experience, that I have redemption through Thy blood, the forgiveness of my sins, according to the riches of Thy grace. Let my conscience be purged from dead works, that I may serve the living God. So shall I rejoice with the felicity of Thy chosen, and the gladness of Thy heritage.

"Thou who didst bleed and die for sinners upon earth, ever livest to make intercession for them in heaven. Thou art therefore able to save to the uttermost. O let me experience the benefit of Thy intercession. Surely Thou art precious to my soul in Thy priestly attire. No hope, no peace, no joy springs up in my bosom, but what is connected with Thy atoning sacrifice, and powerful intercession. Send down Thy blessed Spirit into my heart, to seal me for Thine own: say to my soul, 'I am thy salvation;' then shall I joy in God through Jesus Christ the Lord, the unchangeable and everlasting High Priest of the church, by whom I now receive the atonement."

2. As King in Zion, all power is given to Jesus in heaven and in earth. He has all the dignity, and all the authority of a king. He is the Lawgiver of the church, who is able to save, and to destroy. All acts of worship are to be performed in His name. Ministers preach in His name. Christians pray in His name. Believers are baptized in His name. Christian societies partake of the holy supper in remembrance of Him. Censures on disorderly persons are given to His name. All the officers in His church militant have their commission from Him. And the judgment of the world, at the great day, will be administered by Him, when "he shall sit upon that throne of His glory."

But the Redeemer could not be precious to us in His kingly office, if He were not really and properly God, equal and one with the Father. For, as a learned Divine justly observes, since whatever the Father does in respect to the church is done in and by His Son, if the Son be not possessed of the same properties and perfections with the Father, the foundation of our faith is cast down, and the spring of our consolation utterly stopped. If Christ be no more than man, or a created being, however dignified or exalted, the committing of all rule, authority, and judgment to Him, is so far from being a source of encouragement and comfort, that it may justly be considered as the greatest disadvantage to the church that can be imagined. He who is King in Zion, should be always present with every member of His church; He should know all their hearts, and all their wants; and He should be able to give them immediate relief and protection in every time of danger. This is only possible to Him who is possessed of infinite wisdom, of almighty power, and who is omnipresent, or present in all places at one and the same moment. If Christ be able, at all times, to relieve us, to succour us, to deliver us, and to save us from the power of our spiritual enemies, He is precious to us, while we behold the sceptre of government in His hands. We may then say, "The LORD reigneth, let the earth rejoice, let the multitude of the isles be glad thereof." But if we once suppose that he, of whom it is said, "The government shall be upon His shoulders," is not the Mighty God, or the Lord Jehovah, our faith, our hope, and our joy in Him will be effectually overthrown. We must then hang our harps upon the willows, and give way to all the horrors of despondency and despair.

The rule of Him who is King in Zion, is internal and spiritual. It relates to the minds, the souls, and the consciences of all His subjects. Whatever they do, in a gracious way, either in opposition to sin, or in the discharge of duty, is done under the influence, the guidance, and the support which they receive from Him, in the exercise of His kingly power. His own words corresponding with the constant experience of His people, are a full confirmation of this truth; "Without Me ye can do nothing; that is, nothing successfully, in the Christian warfare. In all the internal actings of their minds, they look unto Jesus, as to one who is more present with their souls, than they are with themselves. And under this consideration He is ever precious to them. But no man can depend on Christ's sovereign power, who is not persuaded, that all His secret groans and sighs, all the inward labourings of His soul against sin, and after a conformity to His image, are immediately and continually under the Redeemer's eye and notice. Whoever dare to deny this great truth, Jesus Christ hath declared that all His churches shall be convinced of it. "For I will make all the churches know that I search the heart, and try the reins of men." And the apostle has assured us, that "all things are naked and open to the eyes of Him with whom we have to do." Without a full persuasion of this, there can be neither faith in His name, love to His person, dependence on His power, nor obedience to His authority.[29] But to you that believe the truth concerning Him, He is precious.

The day is approaching, when the Lord Jesus Christ will openly, in the face of the whole assembled world, vindicate the honour of His kingly government. God has appointed a day in which He will judge the world in righteousness, by that man whom He hath ordained. For the Father judgeth no man, but hath committed all judgment to the Son; that all men should honour the Son, even as they honour the Father. And it is highly proper, as Dr. Smith observes, that this holy and Divine Person, who was buffeted and affronted, condemned and crucified, by an ungrateful and injurious world, should then judge His judges, and be as far advanced above the highest pinnacle of human greatness, as He was once below it. It is fit that Herod may see that he persecuted, not the infant king of a petty province, but the Sovereign of angels and men; and that Pilate and the Jews may be convinced, that He whom they called a

---

29   See *Dr. Owen*, on the Person of Christ.

king in scorn, is really an Emperor, infinitely greater than Caesar; the King of kings, and the Lord of lords for ever and ever.

3. He is precious as the great Prophet of His church. In consequence of man's apostacy from his Maker, the world is involved in darkness. Till we are enlightened by the wisdom which cometh from above, we sit in the region and shadow of death. We are alienated from the life of God, through the ignorance which is in us, and because of the blindness of our hearts. That men are insensible of their native blindness, is but a farther proof of the reality of it. For the natural man receiveth not the things of the Spirit of God, neither can he know them, because they are spiritually discerned. All who are taught of God, learn to know their own ignorance, and consequently they are led to put a just value on the teachings and guidance of Jesus Christ, in His prophetic office.

The glad tidings of pardon, of peace, and reconciliation with God, come by Him. The gospel of salvation is the gospel of Christ. He preached this gospel Himself when on earth. " He hath anointed me," said Jesus, "to preach good tidings to the meek." The ministrations of His servants in every age, whereby they instrumentally turn men from darkness to light, are all by the appointment of Christ, in the fulfillment of His prophetic office.

Nay, the same may be said of all the precious instructions contained in the Scriptures of truth; and therefore the sacred writings are emphatically called "The word of Christ," which should dwell richly in us. Whatever has been revealed unto men, of the mind and will of God, from the beginning of time, has been revealed by Him in the execution of that office, concerning which we now speak. Hence He Himself hath said, "All things are delivered unto Me of My Father; and no man knoweth who the Father is, but the Son, and he to whom the Son will reveal Him." He is the Light of the world, the glorious Sun, in whom all the rays of divine and intellectual light are concentred. "All the treasures of wisdom and knowledge are hid in Him." How precious then must He be in His prophetic office! It is on this account, I presume, among others, that He is so often called by that name, which no one but Himself can bear, THE WORD OF GOD.

The Father solemnly pointed Him out to men, as their prophet, when He sojourned upon earth, by an audible voice from heaven, saying, "This is My beloved Son, hear ye Him." With convincing evidence and authority He has revealed to the world the secrets which lay hid in the Divine mind. He brought His doctrine from the bosom of the Father, according to the declaration of the evangelist John, "The only-begotten Son, who is in the bosom of the Father, He hath declared Him." Jesus tells us, that the words which the Father gave Him, He gave unto us, and that He spake to us that which He had seen with the Father. No wonder therefore is it, that the following awful declaration is made concerning Him, "It shall come to pass, that every soul which will not hear this prophet, shall be destroyed from among the people."

That spiritual illumination, by which sinners are brought to the saving knowledge of God, and of the way of peace, is granted unto them by Jesus Christ as the prophet of His church. He gives unto them the Spirit of truth, to convince them of sin, of righteousness, and of judgment, and to guide them into all truth. As many as are led by the Spirit of God, are the Sons of God; but if any man, in this sense, have not the Spirit of Christ, he is none of His. How necessary, how important, and consequently, how precious are His divine illuminations! By them we are favoured with that knowledge of God, and of the Mediator, which is life eternal.

How greatly endeared then should Jesus Christ be unto us, as our prophet! He who lay in the bosom of the Father has made a fuller and brighter discovery to us what He is, in His admirable and glorious perfections, than we can learn from any other. The light of nature dictates many things to us concerning Him, and the ancient prophets have given us farther information. But none to whom the Father so as the Son does, and those to whom the Son will reveal Him. The knowledge He has of the Father, far transcends the ideas and conceptions of the wisest man that ever existed in the world. He was sent down from heaven to bring life and immortality to light, to reveal the will and the glories of the Father, to make Him appear infinitely lovely and desirable in the eyes of sinners, by representing Him in all the wonders of His compassion, and forgiving mercy. That great, that just, and holy Being is lovely and amiable in the sight of guilty creatures, when He appears as reconciling the world unto Himself, by His Son Jesus Christ, not imputing their trespasses unto them. The great Prophet has informed us, what were the eternal counsels of His Father's love, and what kind designs He formed for our recovery from sin and ruin, when, in His own foreknowledge, He beheld us fallen and miserable. He has told us, what provision the Father made for us, by committing us to the hands of His Son, to be redeemed and saved by Him. It is He who has informed us, that "God so loved the world, as to give His only-begotten Son, that whosoever believeth in Him should not perish, but have eternal life." Whatever was spoken to men in former ages, by angels and by prophets, concerning the great salvation, Jesus has confirmed; and He has added many rich and precious promises of a glorious resurrection, and a future state, and set them before us in a divine light, beyond what either prophets or angels ever revealed.[30]

How happy are they whom He calls out of darkness into His marvelous light; He adopts them into His family, and conforms them to His blessed image.

He continues to supply them with light and life; He guides them with His counsel, and afterwards receives them to glory.

---

30   Dr. Watts.

4. He is the Shepherd of His flock, to conduct, guard and defend them, to feed them in the green pastures of His grace, to cure and heal their diseases, to restore them when they wander, to gather the lambs with His arm, to carry them in His bosom, and gently to lead those that are with young. His power, His care and compassion are infinite. His followers are as sheep in the midst of wolves. We hear one of them saying, "My soul is among lions." These lions may gape and roar, they may seek to devour, but the sheep are safe in the Almighty Shepherd's hands; for He hath said, "I know My sheep, they follow Me, and I give unto them eternal life; and they shall never perish, neither shall any pluck them out of My hand." Such a Shepherd must be precious.

5. He is the Redeemer of their souls, and under that consideration unspeakably precious. The price which He paid for their ransom was not corruptible things, as silver and gold, but His own precious blood: a price of infinite value. The redemption which He hath wrought out is the fruit of His amazing love; it is free, it is every way complete, and it is everlasting; for He hath obtained eternal redemption for us.

When Titus, the Roman emperor, delivered the Enslaved Greeks from their bondage, he was endeared to them in such a manner, that all the night long they celebrated the honour of their deliverer with music and dancing, crying out in raptures of delight, as they surrounded his tent, 'A saviour! a saviour!' But as the redemption obtained by Christ is infinitely more important than the deliverance granted by that noble and victorious prince, it demands still more elevated returns of gratitude, love and praise.

"Christ hath redeemed us from the curse of the law." This could be done no other way, but by His standing in our place, and enduring what we deserved; or, as it is more emphatically expressed by the apostle, "by being made a curse for us."[31] He

---

31 "This," says *Dr. South*, "is spoken so plain and loud, by the universal voice of the

suffered, who was innocent, that we, who are guilty, might escape. He subjected Himself to that very sentence which the law denounced upon us. For it is written, "Cursed is every one that continueth not in all things." Now if Christ endured that very curse which we deserved, that by this means He might deliver us from condemnation, it is evident that He suffered in our stead.

This was absolutely necessary, according to the tenor of the first covenant. For, as God had absolutely declared, "In the day that thou eatest (of the forbidden fruit) thou shalt surely die," no second Adam could restore the ruins of the first, but and taking this curse upon Himself. The truth and justice of the Most High stood absolutely engaged to execute the threatening.

> *Die man, or justice must; unless for Him*
> *Some other able, and as willing, pay*
> *The rigid satisfaction, death for death.*

6. He is, The Everlasting Father. How venerable and amiable, how awful, and yet how endearing is the character of a Father! It commands reverence, and softens that reverence into endearment. It awes, and yet it cheers the mind. It inspires the heart with holy boldness, and fills it with delight and joy. Among men,

---

whole book of God, that Scripture must be *crucified* as well as Christ, to give any other tolerable sense of the expressions."

Some of those who deny the substitution of Christ in the room of sinners, are professed admirers of the *Roman* poet *Virgil*. That poet, who was not perhaps inferior to any heathen writer in the correctness of his style, and the refinement of his taste, represents one man as saved by the wounds and living by the death of another; the one suffers what must otherwise have fallen on the other. Mezentius, when his son interposing in his behalf, was slain by *Æneas*, says,

> —Pro me hostili paterer succedere dextræ
> Quem genui? Tuane hæc genitor per vulnera servor?
> Morte tua vivens:

> —And have I liv'd to see
> My dear-lov'd offspring bleed to rescue me?
> To see my son, and such a son, resign
> His life a ransom for preserving mine?

a wise, a prudent, a tender, and an affectionate father is truly an exalted character. What will not such a father do for the children of his bosom, who look up to him for support, for protection, for instruction, and for comfort?

With what pleasing sensations may we contemplate our Lord Jesus Christ, as a Father! He often when among His disciples on earth, addressed them not only as children, but endearingly called them *little* children. As a father pitieth his children, so the Lord pitieth them that fear Him; for He knoweth our frame, He remembereth that we are dust. We see all, and more than all the tenderness of a Father in the following words, "Is Ephraim My dear son? Is he a pleasant child? For since I spake against him, I do earnestly remember him still; wherefore My bowels are troubled for him: I will surely have mercy on him saith the Lord."

7. He is the bridegroom of His church, and so unspeakably excellent in that view, that neither heaven nor earth can shew such another. We were deformed, polluted, and, in every respect, unworthy of standing in so near and intimate a relation to Him. There was no excellency in us, to render us desirable in His eyes, but every thing to provoke His resentment. And yet He was resolved to betroth us to Himself for ever, in loving-kindness, in faithfulness, and in mercy.

Sin had reduced us to a state of absolute beggary, want, and wretchedness; yet it was His good pleasure to take us into union with Himself, that we might be interested in His unsearchable riches. Nay, though He was rich, for our sakes He became poor, that we through His poverty, might be made rich.

Do we speak of the Bridegroom's love? It is absolutely without parallel. There is nothing of the kind among men which will bear any comparison with it. Though it is immutable in itself, yet in the progressive discoveries of it, it is like the waters in Ezekiel's vision, increasing and rising from the ankles to the knees, from the knees to the loins, till at length it becomes as waters to swim in; a river, a boundless ocean of love. Its height and depth, its length and breadth are immeasurable; it passeth the knowledge of men or angels. It is stronger than death; for Christ loveth His church, and gave Himself for it. In its commencement, it is from everlasting: in its continuance, it endureth for ever. The pattern of it, is the Father's love to His dear Son: Jesus Himself says to those who, according to the language of inspiration, are married unto Him, "As the Father hath loved Me, so have I loved you." The love of the nearest relations among men falls inconceivably short of setting forth the nature, or the ardency of this love. No husband loves the wife of his bosom as Christ loveth His church.

Believers, by their union with Him, are advanced to great riches and honours. God is their Father. They are heirs of God, and joint-heirs with Christ. The riches of eternity are their own. They are taken from the dust and the dunghill, and set among princes, even the princes of His people. The angels in heaven think it no dishonour to be their servants; for they are all ministering spirits, sent forth to minister to the heirs of salvation.

"Thy Maker is thy Husband, the Lord of Hosts is His name." The contract is made, and it will be consummated at the great day, when the marriage-supper will be celebrated with solemnity, triumph, and glory suited to the dignity of the Bridegroom. "Blessed are they who are called to the marriage-supper of the Lamb."

Without enlarging on other particulars, I may observe in general, that to those who believe in Him to the saving of the soul, He is precious under every consideration. He is the bread of God coming down from heaven, and giving everlasting life to their souls. By Him they are really, constantly, daily supported, fed and sustained; and as bread is sweet and precious to a hungry man, so is Christ to those who live by Him. The entertainment He gives to them is a divine, a spiritual feast. "Christ, our passover, is sacrificed for us, therefore let us keep the feast."

He is to them the Sun of Righteousness; the beams of His grace are healing, enlightening, cheering, and full of consolation. If natural light be sweet, if it be a pleasant thing to behold the sun, how much more pleasant to experience the irradiating influences of the Light of life! "On you that fear My name shall the Sun of Righteousness arise, with healing in His wings."

He is the fountain where they bathe their weary souls, and in which they hope for cleansing from all sin and uncleanness. He is the tree of life, under the shadow of which they sit with great delight, and His fruit is sweet to their taste. He is a rock, a strong tower, a hiding-place, where they find protection from every storm and security from every foe. He was precious to the Psalmist under all these views. "I will love Thee, O Lord, my strength. The Lord is my rock, and my fortress, and my deliverer, my God, my strength in whom I trust; my buckler, and the horn of my salvation, and my high tower."

All the strength of believers, all their light, their life, their consolation, and their joy are in Him, from Him, and by Him. Through Him they are brought into the nearest alliance and friendship with God, the firmest union, and the sweetest communion with Him that they are capable of enjoying in the present state, and they shall be introduced into the presence of His glory in the world to come.

It is therefore the business of their lives to know Him to love and honour Him with their whole hears, and to aspire after conformity to His blessed image, and His holy will. They are the circumcision who worship God in the spirit, rejoice in Christ Jesus, and have no confidence in the flesh.

"O blessed Redeemer, I find in Thee all that of which my poor helpless soul stands in need. Though I have the greatest reason for shame and humiliation, on account of what I am in myself, yet in Thee I behold every thing to elevate my hopes, and to afford me relief and encouragement. May my soul magnify the Lord, and my spirit rejoice in God my Saviour! The characters and relations in which Thou hast revealed Thyself to me in Thy word, exhibit a balm for every wound, a cordial for every fear. If I am naked, Thou art the Lord my righteousness; if I am sick, Thou art my physician; if I am weak and helpless, Thou art my strength; if I am neglected and despised, Thou art my compassionate and faithful friend; if I am ignorant, Thou art made unto me wisdom; if I am polluted and enslaved, Thou art made unto me sanctification and redemption; if I am nothing but emptiness and vanity, thou art full of grace and truth."

> *O if I had a thousand tongues,*
> *And could be heard from pole to pole,*
> *I would to all the list'ning world*
> *Declare Thy goodness to my soul.*

SECTION 5

HIS BLOOD AND RIGHTEOUSNESS ARE PRECIOUS.

The complete atonement which Jesus Christ has made for our sins, by the sacrifice of Himself, is the life of the evangelical system, and that which endears it so much to the hearts of them that believe. Here we see pardon procured, and the sinner saved, while sin is condemned and punished; the most awful display of justice and holiness, in conjunction with the freest exercise of mercy; rebels delivered from deserved punishment, and advanced to a state of dignity and honour; and at the same time, the rights of that divine government against which they had rebelled, inviolably preserved and maintained. Through what Jesus Christ has done and suffered for us, we behold the righteous law of God magnified, in justifying those who had violated its precepts, and brought themselves under its curse. In the death of that Lamb of God which taketh away the sin of the world, we perceive at once, the Almighty's eternal abhorrence of that which is evil, and His infinite love to His offending creatures.

We see how precious this subject was to the apostle Paul: "What things were gain to me, those I counted loss for Christ. Yea doubtless, and I count all things but loss, for the excellency of the knowledge of Christ Jesus my Lord: for whom I have suffered the loss of all things, and do count them but dung that I may win Christ, and be found in Him, not having mine own righteousness which is of the law, but that which is through the faith of Christ, the righteousness which is of God by faith." He was struck with a kind of horror at the thought of making any thing the ground of His joy or triumph, but the complete work of Jesus, which He finished on the cross: "God forbid that I should glory, save in the cross of our Lord Jesus Christ.' While others consider Christianity only as an improvement of natural religion, containing a more refined system of morality, he represents it as the religion suitable for sinners, revealing a method of salvation for the guilty, the helpless, and the miserable. "This is a faithful saying, and worthy of all acceptation, that Jesus Christ came into the world to save sinners." His fellow-labourers heartily concurred with him in this: for, says he, "*We* preach Christ crucified."

To a condemned malefactor, a pardon sent from his offended sovereign must be precious. So, nothing can be matter of greater comfort in this world than to know that we have redemption through the blood of Jesus, the forgiveness of our sins, according to the riches of His grace. As soon may light and heat be separated from the beams of the sun, as peace and consolation from the voice of pardon. Hence when our Lord sojourned on earth, the relief which He administered to the distressed was generally comprehended in these words, "Son, daughter, be of good cheer; thy sins are forgiven thee."

The blood of our Divine Saviour is emphatically called *precious blood*. The shedding of His blood was the finishing act of His obedience to the law, as our surety, in our room and stead. It procures our pardon, our peace with God, and our everlasting salvation. "Being justified by His blood, we shall be saved from wrath through Him."

What He did and suffered was not on His own account, but on account of those whom He came to save. To consider Him simply as an individual, is highly injurious to His character, as Mediator. The ideas of substitution and imputation are necessarily included in that character; the imputation of our sins to *Him*, and of His righteousness to *us*. Without admitting these considerations, the sufferings which Christ underwent, had they been greater than they were, could avail us nothing, But the divine word assures us, that "as by the offence of one, judgment came upon all men to condemnation, so by the obedience of one (Jesus Christ) many are made righteous." We are made the righteousness of God *in Him*, as He wrought out that righteousness by which we are justified, not only in our nature, but in our name, considered as our Head and Representative. Without admitting the idea of substitution, there is no more ground for reliance on the obedience of Christ, than for reliance on the obedience of an angel.

This truth, being of the greatest importance to our relief and comfort, is set forth in the clearest light by the sacred writers. They assure us, that in our Redeemer, personally considered, there was no sin, neither was guile found in His mouth; He was holy, harmless, undefiled, separate from sinners. "Yet it pleased the Lord to bruise Him; He was smitten of God and afflicted;" but on what account? "All we like sheep have gone astray; we have turned every one to his own way; and the Lord hath laid on Him the iniquity of us all. He was wounded for our transgressions, He was bruised for our iniquities: the chastisement of our peace was upon Him, and with His stripes we are healed." Hence His obedience unto death is the only ground of our hope and joy. "We joy in God through Jesus Christ our Lord, by whom we have now received the atonement." We look to Calvary, and view the suffering Saviour, as bearing our sins, in His own body on the tree, and putting them away by the sacrifice of Himself. Believing the salutary truth, an acquittal from guilt and condemnation is announced to our consciences, and we are filled with the peace of God.

We see that, through what Jesus Christ has done and suffered, as our substitute, that holy law which we have broken is highly honoured; and that awful justice which we have provoked is completely satisfied. His obedience in life, His obedience unto death, and His obedience in death, is sometimes in Scripture, by a usual figure, called His blood, His precious blood, and the blood of God; at other times it is expressed by the term righteousness; the righteousness of God, which is unto all and upon all them that believe. It is evident that the different terms mean one and the same thing, the complete work of the great Surety on our account, and in our stead.

That obedience, which Jesus thus performed, is every way as excellent as eternal wisdom itself could devise, and as perfect as divine rectitude could require. The Father declares Himself well pleased with it. All the divine attributes are glorified by it, while it fully answers every saving purpose to those that believe, and ensures the richest blessings unto them, both in this world, and that which is to come. On all which accounts it is unspeakably precious. The evangelical prophet, personating the whole church, triumphs in it in the following manner: "I will greatly rejoice in the Lord, my soul shall be joyful in my God: for He hath clothed me with the garments of salvation, He hath covered me with the

robe of righteousness, as a bridegroom decketh himself with ornaments, and as a bride adorneth herself with jewels."

SECTION 6

HIS LOVE IS PRECIOUS

This is the most powerful inducement that can be proposed to
us, to excite our ardent affections towards the gracious Redeemer.
Neither the reasonings of philosophers, the persuasions of ora-
tors, nor even the displays of divine goodness in the works of creation and providence, will answer this end, if our hearts are proof
against the attractions of a Saviour's love. Can we contemplate
the agonies He endured for us, and thus place ourselves under the
beams of His unparalleled love, and not feel in our melting hearts
some returns of affection and regard for Him!

The apostle John speaks very justly, when he says, "We loved
Him because He first loved us." And another apostle makes use
of very strong terms when treating on the same subject, "The love
of Christ," says he, "constraineth us." The love of Jesus was most
strongly manifested in His dying for us. What can be expected
to attract our love, if this do not? He Himself speaks of it as that
which should be efficacious in winning the hearts of men; "And I,
if I be lifted up from the earth will draw all men unto Me."

They who are inattentive to the compassion of a dying Redeemer, lose the strongest motive to love and obedience. They are
acting the part of the foolish Galatians, who were carried away
from this glorious subject, by a kind of infatuation. "O foolish Galatians, who hath bewitched you that ye should not obey
the truth, before whose eyes Jesus Christ hath been evidently set
forth, crucified among you." O how desirable is it to be enabled
constantly to behold Him by faith as crucified for us! Surely we
should never forget, that, when He might have left us to perish,

such was His love, He died that we might live, He endured the greatest agonies, that He might snatch us from the jaws of destruction, and open to us the gates of everlasting peace and felicity. Well may such a Saviour be precious to us. Surely they who love Him most, have reason still to be grieved that they do not love Him more.

He hath loved us so as to ransom us with His blood; ransom us from a voluntary bondage; from a captivity the most vile and miserable; a captivity from which nothing but Almighty grace could have set us free. Could we have made any pretence to merit, the case had been different. But since we were totally unworthy, entirely helpless, wretched and undone, human vanity is for ever silenced, and boasting eternally excluded. It was the good pleasure of Him that saves us, to love us freely.

It is this grace which tunes the harps of heaven, and affords the saints in light a never-failing subject of harmony and praise. On this theme the spirits of just men made perfect fix their meditations. They admire the glorious mystery of the victorious cross, and sing the wonders of redeeming love.

This love is celebrated by them with peculiar praises; "They sang a new song, saying, 'Thou art worthy to take the book, and open the seals thereof, for Thou wast slain and hast redeemed us to God by Thy blood, out of every kingdom, and tongue, and people, and nation.' And I beheld, and I heard the voice of many angels round about the throne, and the living creatures, and the elders; and the number of them was ten thousand times ten thousand, and thousands of thousands; saying with a loud voice, 'Worthy is the Lamb that was slain, to receive power, and riches, and wisdom, and strength, and honour, and glory, and blessing.' "

What is most wonderful of all is, that Jesus should shew such love as this for *sinful* men, for men who were the enemies of God. "While we were enemies, we were reconciled to God by the death of His Son." His love to them was dying love, and in this the greatness of it most of all appears. When in His agony He sweat great drops of blood falling down to the ground, it was for enemies. The shame and spitting to which He meekly submitted, the torments inflicted on His body, and the inexpressible sorrows which overwhelmed His soul, were all endured for enemies, to save them from ruin, and to exalt them to glory and felicity. It was for them that He submitted to have the arrows of Divine vengeance spent upon Him, which occasioned His bloody sweat, and His awful out-cry upon the cross, "My God, My God, why hast Thou forsaken Me?" His vitals were rent, His heart was broken; according to the Divine prediction, it melted like was in the midst of His bowels. Probably, through violent fermentation, the crimson fluid became a mixture of blood and water, partly issuing from the pores of His body in the garden, and partly flowing from His side, when pierced by the spear; "Forthwith there came out blood and water." He endured all this for the honour of Divine justice, or to take away the dishonour which we have done to God by our sins, and so to commend or set forth His love to us, in the most striking manner possible.

Oh! for this love let rocks and hills
Their lasting silence break,
And all harmonious human tongues
The Saviour's praises speak.

He suffered from the hand of justice as if His demerits had been infinite, though He was holy, harmless, and undefiled. The reason was, "The Lord hath laid on Him the iniquity of us all. Therefore He was stricken, smitten of God, and afflicted." It was for our transgressions that He was wounded; it was for our iniquities that He was bruised. Our peace is procured by His chastisement, and our healing by His stripes. If such a Saviour is not precious to us, nothing can equal our ingratitude. He died for those who spilt His blood, and who mocked Him in the midst of His severest agonies, as is evident from His intercession for them; "Father, forgive them, they know not what they do." O Thou loving Saviour! It is meet and right that every knee in heaven and earth should bow to Thee, and that every angel, and every saint should love Thee, and adore Thee for ever! O my soul,

> —*Survey the wond'rous cure,*
> *And at each step let higher wonders rise.*
> *Pardon for infinite offence! And pardon*
> *Through means which speak its value infinite!*
> *A pardon bought with blood!—With blood divine!*
> *With blood divine of Him I made my foe!—*
> *Persisted to provoke!—Though woo'd and aw'd*
> *Blest and chastis'd a flagrant rebel still;—*
> *Nor I alone! A rebel universe!*
> *My species up in arms!—Not one exempt!*
> *Yet for the foulest of the foul He dies!*

The gracious manifestations of His love to our souls are exceedingly precious. "There are many that say, 'Who will shew us any good?' But, Lord lift Thou up the light of Thy countenance upon us! This will put gladness into our hearts more than the increase of corn, or wine, or oil. The favour is life, yea, Thy loving-kindness is better than life itself."

"O blessed Jesus, Thy love is wonderful! It is the admiration of angels, the joy and song of glorified saints. The experimental sense of it on earth sweetens the bitterness of life, and disarms death of all its terrors! It was love that moved Thee to bow the heavens, to come down and sojourn on earth, to humble Thyself, to take on Thee the form of a servant, and become obedient unto death, even the death of the cross. Thou didst pity me in my lost estate; Thou didst find me when I sought Thee not; Thou didst speak peace to me in the day of my distress, when the clouds of guilt and darkness hung heavy on my soul, and I was brought to

the borders of despair. Thou hast borne with all my weakness, corrected my mistakes, restored me from my wanderings, and healed
my backslidings. May Thy loving-kindness be ever before mine
eyes, to induce me to walk in Thy truth. May it be the daily theme
of my mediations, and the constant joy of my heart.

When I am favoured with the light of Thy countenance, and
the comfortable sense of Thy love, my soul is filled and satisfied.
All the glories of the world are then darkened, and turned into
deformity. They are but broken cisterns; Thou art the fountain of
living waters. The streams of created enjoyments are shallow and
deceitful as a brook; but Thou art the full ocean of never-failing
delight and satisfaction.

"To Thy love I must ascribe my whole salvation; and through
all the ages of a blissful eternity, I humbly hope and trust, I shall
proclaim the wonders of redeeming love, and tell to listening angels what this love has done for my soul. "Unto Him that loved
us, and washed us from our sins in His own blood, and hath made
us kings and priests to God and His Father, to Him be glory and
dominion for ever and ever. Amen."

SECTION 7

HIS THRONE IS PRECIOUS

The men of the world are totally ignorant of that Delightful intercourse which is carried on between Christians and their
exalted and interceding Saviour; what petitions they daily present
before His throne, and what gracious answers they receive from
Him. The eyes of the Lord are upon the righteous, and His ears
are ever open to their cries. Whoever may overlook or disappoint
them, He will not. When their spirits are overwhelmed within
them, He knoweth their path. When human means and efforts
fail, when every thing looks dark before them, when their way

seems to be shut up on every side, and they are brought to the lowest ebb, still they have welcome access to the Divine throne, where they may tell all their wants, and unbosom their cares and sorrows, with the certain hope of obtaining mercy, and finding grace to help in the time of need.

Prayer is not only a duty but an inestimable privilege. The condescension of God is wonderful in lending His gracious ear to sinful worms. When the heart of a Christian is under a proper influence, he finds a greater pleasure in approaching the Divine throne, than in any thing this world can afford. He obtains more light, strength, comfort and refreshment by one hour's converse with God, than he could do by any other means.

The prophet Daniel fully shewed how precious the throne of grace was to him, since neither the prohibition of the king, nor the threatened horrors of the den of lions, could prevail with him to omit one opportunity of approaching it.

What an unspeakable privilege is it to have liberty of access to God! To have His permission, nay, His invitation and command, to come boldly to His throne of grace, and to call Him our Father in Christ! Amidst surrounding dangers, snares and temptations, we may fly to Him as our refuge, and lift up our hearts to Him in fervent and earnest prayer. To Him we may tell all our inmost cares, and open all our griefs. His ears are always attentive to our requests, and the gales of His blessed Spirit will dispel the gloom in which we are involved, and breathe internal peace and fragrance on our souls.

In the exercises of retired devotion, we may cherish and express all the holy affections of our souls, with the greatest freedom. We may say a thousand things to our heavenly Father in secret, which would not be proper in public devotion. We may pour out our souls before Him, in the strongest and most pathetic sentiments of holy desire, and divine delight. We may tell Him all the disquietudes of our consciences, the secret anguish and shame of our hearts, because of those offences which are known to Him alone; we may sigh deeply, and pour out the tear of penitence into His bosom. We may tell Him how intense our desires are to be assured of His love, and to be conformed to His image. We may rejoice in His sight with divine exultation and holy triumph, in the prospect of being shortly with Him in the upper world.

Let the favourites of an earthly prince value themselves on being permitted to hold converse with their sovereign, I would ever esteem it a privilege infinitely superior, to have free and welcome access to the King of kings.

SECTION 8

THE DOCTRINE OF CHRIST IS PRECIOUS.

The truths of the gospel reveal a method of salvation every way honourable to God and His righteous government, and every way suitable to our necessities. The ground, the substance, and the spirit of the glad tidings sent from heaven to a lost world are, that Jesus Christ died for our sins, according to the Scriptures. The apostle Paul was determined, as a minister, to know nothing save Jesus Christ, and Him crucified. This theme, and the truths connected with it, engrossed all His thoughts. He dwelt so much upon these subjects, that it might appear as if he knew nothing else, and is if nothing else were, comparatively speaking, worthy of His attention.

When our Lord, after His resurrection, honoured His disciples with His company in their journey to Emmaus, He began at Moses and all the prophets, and expounded to them in all the Scriptures, the things concerning Himself. Did they hear the Divine truths He advanced with indifference? Far from it. These truths were precious to their souls, as appears from their own animated expressions; "Did not our hearts burn within us while He talked with us by the way, and opened to us the Scriptures?"

The word of Christ in general is precious to those that believe. The coin of Caesar bore His image and superscription, so the Divine word bears the image of Christ, and consequently must be dear to those who love Him. They revere that sacred injuction, "Let the word of Christ dwell in you richly, in all wisdom, that ye may be able also to admonish one another."

David, the king of Israel made while living, this public declaration, and left it, when he died, to be observed by all succeeding generations, that the word of God was better to him than thousands of gold and silver; that it was sweeter to him than honey, or the honey-comb; and that it was his meditation all the day. If he tasted so much sweetness in the least valuable part of the Divine word, how much richer is the feast to us in these latter days! Since the gospel is now added to the law; the Lord has put His last hand to the work, has "sealed up the sun and rendered it full of wisdom and perfect in beauty."

The divine Redeemer cannot, in this world, be seen face to face. This is the felicity of the heavenly state. But in His holy word, as in a glass, we behold His glory. The lineaments of His beauty are here drawn by a divine pencil. The Bible must consequently be a precious book in the estimation of every Christian.

This inestimable book unfolds to our view the path of peace, the way everlasting. We here learn how the guilty may be pardoned, in perfect consistency with the honour of infinite holiness; how God can be just, and the justifier of the ungodly, who, in themselves deserve everlasting condemnation. We are indebted to this sacred volume for all the light that ever chased the glooms of doubts, or cheered the bosom of despondency; for all that gives confidence to faith, energy to hope, ardency to love, or fervour to devotion; for whatever can tranquillize the mind in life, or administer consola-

tion at the last hour. We have here the doctrine which is according
to godliness; we have here the words of everlasting life.

> *The volume of my Father's grace*
> *Does all my grief assuage;*
> *Here I behold my Saviour's face,*
> *Almost in ev'ry page.*

The general design of this divine book is, to establish the soul
in believing the testimony which God has given concerning His
Son Jesus Christ, to direct it in doing His will, and to comfort it
in all the sufferings and afflictions attendant on the present state.
The sacred volume therefore insists much on faith, obedience, and
patience. The first is certainly the ground-work of the other two.

Holy men of God, whose sentiments and experiences are here
left upon record, have given us the most magnificent eulogiums
of this word. They represent it as a source of felicity. They tell
us, that it converts and restores the soul; that it gives wisdom
to the simple; that it is more to be desired than the richest treasures, or the sweetest enjoyments this world can afford; that it is
adapted to instruct, to correct, to comfort, and to render the man
of God perfect. They assure us, that these are not mere fancies,
destitute of sense and truth; the inspired witnesses unitedly testify,
that they themselves have known the power of the divine word by
their own experience; that when they have made it the subject of
their attentive meditation, they have been "satisfied as with mar-
row and fatness, and have rejoiced in it more than they that find
great spoil."

To expatiate on the several doctrines contained in the Bible,
and to point out the preciousness of each, is not my present design. It may suffice to say, that they all centre in Christ Jesus, and
are all valuable in the estimation of His people on that account.
Does this precious book speak of the love of God, the source of
all good to man? It is in Christ Jesus. Does it unfold the ancient

counsels of infinite wisdom and grace? They are the eternal purposes of the Father in Christ Jesus our Lord. Does it speak of redemption? It is by His blood—of justification. It is through His righteousness—of conversion. We are called by His grace—of regeneration. We are quickened together with Christ—of adoption. We are the children of God, by faith in Jesus Christ—of perseverance. Because He lives, we shall live also—of eternal glory. It is the gift of God through our Lord Jesus Christ.

How divinely excellent are these sacred truths! With what sovereign efficacy do they operate upon the mind and heart, when accompanied by the agency of the blessed Spirit! How powerfully do they awaken repentance, and melt the soul into holy sorrow! In what an illustrious light do they represent the majesty and the grace of the blessed God, and how do they command our humble adoration! How do they display the wonders of His wisdom, and the riches of His mercy in Christ Jesus, to produce faith, and attract desire and love! What a blessed foundation do they lay for and infinite variety of devout inferences, and pathetic admonitions, suited to every case! These divine truths relieve the soul under every distress; that by patience and comfort of the Scriptures we may have hope towards God. The believer lives on the divine variety of salutary and transporting objects set before him in the sacred pages. Here he finds the fountains of life set open, every stream flowing with holiness and consolation. It is His prevailing desire, that all His affections may be under the command and influence of the divine word, that while it affords him intense delight, it may animate him to active zeal in the practice of every thing which it enjoins, teaching him to deny ungodliness and worldly lusts, and to live soberly, righteously, and godly in this present world, while he looks for the blessed hope, in that which is to come.

A certain martyr; who was condemned to die for his inviolable adherence to the doctrines of Scripture, gave this expressive testimony, in his last moments, of his regard for that divine book. Being arrived at the stake, and having composed himself for suffering, he took his final leave of all below, in these affecting words, "Farewell sun and moon! Farewell all the beauties of creation, and all the comforts of life! Farewell my honoured friends! Farewell my beloved relations! And farewell thou Precious book of God!"

SECTION 9

HIS PROMISES ARE PRECIOUS.

These shall stand in force, though heaven and earth shall pass away. Length of time cannot diminish their efficacy, nor alter what the mouth of the Lord hath spoken. The sun may fail to rise, and men expect its returning light in vain, but the promises of everlasting truth cannot be broke. "The mountains shall depart, and the hills be removed; but My kindness shall not depart from thee, neither shall the covenant of My peace be removed, saith the Lord that hath mercy on thee." The course of nature may be reversed, and all be chaos again; but the promises of God cannot fail for evermore, since He that made them is immutable, and cannot by any change deceive the hopes of them that trust in Him. It is impossible that He should promise any thing that it is beyond His ability to perform. He is not as a man that He should lie, nor as the son of man that He should repent. Hath He said, I will surely do thee good, and shall He not do it? Hath He spoken, and shall He not accomplish the thing that is gone out of His lips!

If He speak a promise once,
Th' eternal grace is sure.

Our fathers trusted in Him, and were not confounded, they relied on His faithful word, and were delivered. All the succeeding generations of His people, from the beginning of time, have placed their confidence in what He hath spoken, and none could ever charge Him, either with want of compassion, or breach of truth.

"He hath given unto us exceeding great and precious promises; that by these ye may be partakers of the Divine nature, having escaped the corruption that is in the world through lust." They are *great*, as being made by the Most High God, the Possessor of heaven and earth; and they contain the greatest things that language can express, or thought conceive; deliverance from sin, and all its consequences; the bestowment of all grace here, and of everlasting glory hereafter. "Eye hath not seen, nor ear heard, neither have entered into the heart of man, the things which God hath prepared for them that love Him." The promises are *precious* in their origin, the free and sovereign grace of God; in their nature, as they contain the most precious things; in their suitableness to our case, and to all our wants; and in their efficacy upon our souls; to subdue our fears, to support our faith, to calm our disquietudes, to elevate our hopes, to afford us comfort in all our sorrows, and to transform us into the Divine likeness; for by these promises we are made partakers of the Divine nature.

SECTION 10

THE COMMANDS OF OUR REDEEMER ARE PRECIOUS.

The laws of His mouth are better than thousands of gold and silver. To be under these divine restraints is sweeter than liberty.

A practical regard to the commands of Christ is the best evidence that He is precious to us. It is very remarkable with what emphasis He Himself speaks on this head, how much He insists upon this one article, and how often He repeats it. "If ye love Me, keep My commandments. If a man love Me, He will keep My words. He that loveth Me not, keepeth not My sayings. Every branch in Me that beareth not fruit, He taketh away; and every branch that beareth fruit, He purgeth it. Herein is My Father glorified, that ye bear much fruit; so shall ye be My disciples. Ye are My friends if ye do whatsoever I command you."

A holy conformity to the Divine will is as much the end of all that God does for His people, as fruit is the end of all that the husbandman does about His field or His vineyard. Regard for Christ then is best shewn by obedience to His will. "He that hath My commandments, and keepeth them, he it is that loveth Me." We have the commands of our divine Master; but do we keep them? If ye know these things, happy are ye if ye do them. He who is our Redeemer, is also our Lord and Governor. If we have a sincere attachment to Him, we shall be subject to His authority, and take care to please Him. Above all other things we shall be afraid of displeasing and offending Him. Our obedience to Him will be hearty and sincere, constant and impartial. Our miscarriages will fill us with disquietude and sorrow. The genuine language of our hearts will be, O that my ways were directed to keep Thy statutes! Then shall I not be ashamed, when I have respect unto all Thy commandments. One of the disciples of Jesus says, "His commandments are not grievous;" another, "I delight in the law of God after the inward man."

Our regard for His laws is shewn, not only in the sincerity, but in the willingness and cheerfulness of our obedience. Reluctance to His service is inexcusable, weariness and dulness in it shameful. Our obedience should be universal and constant. We should be steadfast and unmoveable, always abounding in the work of the Lord, forasmuch as we know that our labour is not in vain in the Lord.

We are commanded to love the the Author of our being with all our mind, with all our soul, and with all our strength. To love Him with all our mind, is to have the highest esteem of Him, in our judgment, as the most excellent and the best of beings, and as our only all-sufficient good. To love Him with all our soul, is to choose Him for our eternal portion, to give up ourselves to Him as our Lord and Ruler, and to receive Him as our God, and our reconciled Father, according to the discoveries of His grace in Christ Jesus. And to love Him with all our strength, is to worship Him with holy diligence, and, according to the utmost of our capacity and power to do His will, and promote His honour in the world.

The mere flashes of sudden passion, in a devout moment, without a supreme and settled esteem of God in the mind, and a careful and active obedience to His commands, are of little consequence. The hearers who received the word, like seed which fell on stony ground, are said to receive it with joy; but their devotion and religion were only a sudden blaze, which quickly expired. They endured but for a while. On the other hand, they who receive the seed into good ground, are they, who having heard the word, keep it, and bring forth fruit with patience.

"Lord, let my obedience to Thy commands be universal; my whole man being subject to Thy whole will, and that continually and perseveringly, even to the end of life; let it have its root in my heart, that it may not wither like grass which has no deepness of earth, but be like a tree planted by the rivers of water, bringing forth fruit in due season. Let my obedience arise from a holy reverence of Thee, the great Lawgiver; a reverence tempered with love and gratitude. I shall then account none of Thy commands either grievous or unimportant, but esteem them all to be right and precious. Under the influence of the great truths I profess to believe, may the vices of my mind, and the disorders of my life be effectually subdued and corrected, that in righteousness and holiness I may walk before Thee, in the land of the living. Engrave Thy law on the fleshly table of my heart, that I may love it exceedingly; then my constant study and endeavour will be to exhibit a copy of it in the various actions of my life. Then shall I not be ashamed when I have respect unto all Thy commandments; in keeping of them there is great reward."

SECTION 11

HIS WAYS ARE PRECIOUS.

When we are enabled, in sincerity, to make choice of our Lord Jesus Christ, as our Prophet, our priest, and our king, we feel the force of our obligations to Him, we see the beauty and honour of His service, and are convinced that nothing is worthy, in any sense, to stand in competition with it. And in proportion as He is precious to us, His ways and His service will be pleasant; so that we shall do the will of God from the heart.

Those whom our Lord Jesus Christ has purified unto Himself, as His peculiar people, are zealous of good works. They give up themselves to His service, and make it their principal business to please Him, and to live to Him. Their Christian course is compared to those exercises in which men exert their strength, and that with the greatest earnestness and eagerness; particularly running, wrestling, and fighting.

Where love to Jesus reigns in the heart, it will induce a man to act in a manner suitable to it. Supreme love, as an excellent writer has observed, governs all the active train of human passions, and leads them, in sweet captivity, to cheerful obedience. And as the inward affections will be thus engaged towards the Redeemer, the outward powers will be employed in corresponding exercises. The way in which we are to shew that Jesus is precious to us, is by walking in His truth, and fulfilling every present duty with delight. It is then that we find the ways of wisdom to be ways of pleasantness, and all her paths to be paths of peace. Love to Jesus Christ induces us to account every duty a privilege, and to esteem the service of our Divine Master perfect freedom.

There is nothing in the ways of religion that ought to be deemed burdensome. To walk in them with fervour and spirituality of mind, and with regularity, integrity, and circumspection, has a tendency to make us calm, easy, and happy. The yoke of Christ is an easy, not a galling yoke. The more we wear it, the easier and the pleasanter it is. We should esteem the worship of God as the most needful part of our daily business, and the most delightful part of our daily comforts. His laws are the dictates of the highest wisdom and goodness. It becomes us to rejoice that we are under His government, and to serve Him with the greatest cheerfulness.

The consolations which come from above are Only to be experienced in the ways of religion, and the paths of holiness.[32] And there are no fantastic delusions, but substantial and divine delights; joys with which a stranger intermeddleth not. They serve to enlarge the mind, and give it a more elevated turn, while it derives its sovereign supports from the source of all excellency and perfection, and rests on nothing unworthy the dignity of an immortal soul, on nothing beneath Him who is the Fountain of boundless and immortal felicity.

If Christ be precious to us, we shall have a high value, a sincere regard for those ways in which He has promised His presence with His people. We shall be ready to say with those of ancient times,

---

32 The life of the negligent and loose professor of Christianity, seems to be a perpetual struggle to reconcile impossibilities; it is an endeavour to unite what God has for ever separated, peace and sin; unchristian practices, and Christian comforts; a quiet conscience, and a disorderly life; a heart full of the cares and concerns of the present world, and a well-grounded and cheerful expectation of the happiness of the next. An attempt to unite these is as vain as an endeavour to put asunder what God has joined together.

"In the way of Thy judgments, O God, have we waited for Thee; the desire of our souls is to Thy name, and to the remembrance of Thee. Thou meetest Him that rejoiceth and worketh righteousness; those that remember Thee in Thy ways." When the church desires to know where the good Shepherd feeds His sheep, where He makes His flock to rest at noon, in the heat of the day, she is answered in the following tender and endearing manner; "If thou know not, O thou fairest among women, go thy way forth by the footsteps of the flock, feed thy kids besides the shepherds' tents."

SECTION 12

HIS PEOPLE ARE PRECIOUS.

So dear are the followers of Christ to them that believe, that they are ready and willing to treat such as brethren, to shew kindness and good-will to them on all occasions, and though they be poor and despised in the world, to esteem them as the excellent in the earth, because of their conformity and relation to Christ. We make it manifest that we have a sincere affection to such, when we discover a pitiful and tender spirit towards them in calamity, when we are ready to bear their burdens, and willing to spend part of our substance, and to suffer many inconveniences in our worldly interests, in order to promote their welfare in soul and body.

Consider the example of the apostle Paul. All his epistles abound with expressions of an earnest and overflowing affection to the followers of Christ. He expresses his ardent love to them, by calling them dearly beloved and longed for. He would have them to know the abundant love which He had towards them. He says, "We were gentle among you, even as a nurse cherisheth her children; so, being affectionately desirous of you, we are willing to have imparted unto you, not the gospel of God only, but our own souls also, because ye were dear unto us."

The apostle John, the disciple whom Jesus loved, who was indulged with the sweetest familiarity with Him, and even permitted to lean on His bosom, says more concerning love to the brethren than any other of the apostles. To collect all that he writes on this subject, would be to transcribe a considerable part of his epistles. His addresses to the children of God are exceedingly tender and pathetical, breathing out nothing but the most fervent love. This sweet and holy affection had full possession of his heart, and the expressions of it flowed freely and abundantly from his lips and his pen. He proposes the serious inquiry, "If a man have this world's goods, and seeing his brother have need, shutteth up the bowels of his compassion from him, how dwelleth the love of God in him?" He considers love to the brethren as that by which we may know that we are passed from death unto life.

If we love not our brethren whom we have seen, how can we love God whom we have not seen? All Christ's disciples bear His image; if the original be precious to us, we shall have some regard for the picture, however imperfect it may be in the present state.

The love we are to manifest to the brethren is different, as a sensible writer well observes, from that universal benevolence which we owe to men in general, and to the regard we have for our natural relations in particular. It is an injunction given by our Lord Jesus to His disciples in a special manner, "A new commandment I give *unto you*, that ye love one another." Sometimes it is connected with the command to believe in Jesus; to signify unto us, that without faith in Him we are incapable of loving His followers in a proper manner. "This is His commandment, that we should believe on the name of His Son Jesus Christ, and love one another, as He gave us commandment." The love intended, is a love to those who know the truth, and that for the truth's sake which dwelleth in them. It is far from being confined to any particular party or denomination of Christians, the objects of it are, all of every name, place, or nation, who give evidence of their being saints, and faithful brethren in Christ Jesus.

The motive or reason enforcing this love is, the regard which the Redeemer has to His followers; "As I have loved you, that ye also love one another." To impress this injunction the more, He repeats it, "This is My commandment, that ye love one another, as I have loved you." And He shews in what manner He had loved them, in the words immediately following: "Greater love hath no man than this, that a man lay down his life for his friends." Jesus did more than this, He laid down His life for enemies; but as He is here speaking of love to one another, as friends and brethren, He enforces His injunction by this instance of His love towards them, considered as His friends. And the apostle John, taking up the idea suggested by his divine Master, says, "Hereby perceive we the love of God (the Redeemer) because He laid down His life for us." He also draws the same inference from it which his Master did, with particular application to Himself, and to those whom he addresses: "Beloved, if God (the Redeemer) so loved us, we ought also to love one another; we ought (if called to it) to lay down our lives for the brethren." This is a new motive to brotherly love. A motive peculiar to the gospel; a motive which, in a special manner, respects the friends of Christ, for whom He had so high a degree of regard as to lay down His life in their stead. In the passage cited above, it is supposed, that these friends of Christ, believe the great doctrine of atonement, and that, as such, they should be influenced by it to that mutual affection which is required of them, by Him who ransomed them with His blood.

Obedience to this command of our adorable Saviour, is the grand evidence of our being His true followers; "By this shall all men know that ye are My disciples, if ye have love to one another." Hence it is evident, that the love intended is not a hidden principle in the mind, which discovers not itself in outward acts of kindness; for such a love could not point out the subjects of it to general notice; it must mean an attachment so sincere, so fervent, as to be attended with effects which all men can see; a love which is operative and beneficial; a love in deed and in truth, producing such fruits in all the behaviour of Christians towards one another, as will, in a striking and convincing manner, distinguish them from all the world besides, and mark them out to all observers, as the disciples of a living Saviour.

Nor is this love intended only to produce a conviction in others, that the subjects of it belong to Christ; it is also to be the evidence of the same thing in their own consciences. "We know that we have passed from death unto life, because we love the brethren: he that loveth not his brother abideth in death. My little children (for such ye are to resemble in true simplicity of heart) let us not love in word, neither in tongue (only) but in deed and truth. And hereby we know that we are of the truth, and shall assure our hearts before Him. For if our hearts condemn us (of being destitute of this love) God is greater than our heart, and knoweth all things. Beloved, if our heart condemn us not, then have we confidence towards God."

Obedience to this new commandment of brotherly love is of such importance in the religion of Jesus, that it is evident from the divine word, there is no real Christianity without it; since it is not only represented as the visible distinction between Christ's disciples and the men of the world; as the great evidence of our being born of God, and having a right knowledge of Him; of His dwelling in us, and of our dwelling in Him, as the apostle John shews; but it is one of the principal evidences of what is now under our immediate consideration; namely, of our regard to Christ Himself, or of His being precious to us. "Every one that loveth Him that begat, loveth Him also that is begotten of Him. No man hath seen God at any time; if we love one another, His love is perfected in us." As if it had been said, "The objects of His love, who bear His holy image, are daily before our eyes, that we may have an opportunity of testifying our love to Him, by shewing kindness to them for His sake. If therefore we love one another, our love to the unseen Redeemer produces its proper effect, and is proved to be true and sincere." Without this operative principle of brotherly affection, in vain do we pretend, either that Christ has the chief place in our hearts, or that we are interested in His love to us.

This is that charity concerning which the apostle Paul writes so largely to the Corinthian church. He shews its excellence above the most useful and extraordinary gifts of the Spirit, and declares, that though a man, who is destitute of it, should give all his goods to feed the poor, and his body to be burned, it would profit him nothing. He describes this love, as being directly opposite to every malignant passion and disposition; to pride, selfishness, evil-surmising, and envy. He shews that it is kind, bountiful, and beneficient; engaging the followers of Christ, in every prudent and possible way to serve one another. He intimates, that in the present, imperfect state, it is requisite to use much self-denial in maintaining and manifesting this love, and that it requires the exercise of humility, patience, meekness, and long-suffering, in enduring all trying things, and bearing one another's burdens. But as on the one hand, it rejoiceth not in iniquity, so as to bear with a brother in any gross error, or in any practice contrary to the gospel, but is solicitous to restore such a one, in the spirit of meekness; so, on the other hand, it rejoiceth in the saving truth of Christ, which so gloriously manifests his love to men. The truth of the gospel is one of the first objects of a believer's delight, and his love to the brethren is just in proportion as he perceives the truth to dwell in them, in its power and efficacy; for he loves them "for the truth's sake which dwelleth in them."

IN WHAT RESPECTS 169

This love, when compared with faith and hope, is said to be greater than either of them, and that on two accounts; in the first place it excels them in duration: for when faith and hope shall have issued in the sight and enjoyment of their respective objects, then love will be made perfect, and it will prevail and reign for ever in the regions of unfading felicity. And in the second place, love may be considered as superior to faith and hope, even in the present state, because, in its nature, it is the very image of God. It is one of the principal things wherein the child of grace resembles his heavenly Father, and is conformed to His likeness; for "God is love." It is that in which the believer most imitates the Lord Jesus Christ, in the peculiarly endearing part of his character, his love to men. "Be followers of God as dear children; and walk in love, as Christ hath loved us, and given Himself for us."[33]

To set this article in the most striking point of light imaginable, we are expressly taught, that by this love to the saints, as arising from love to the Saviour's name, He will, when He comes to judge the world at the last day, distinguish His own people from all other. Let the reader attentively consider the account given by the supreme Judge Himself, of what will be the process of that awful day, in the twenty-fifth chapter of the evangelist Matthew. They on the left hand will be condemned, as having given no proof of attachment to Christ, by shewing regard to His followers. While to those on the right hand the great Judge will say, "Come ye blessed of My Father, inherit the kingdom prepared for you, from the foundation of the world; for I was an hungered, and ye gave Me meat; I was thirsty, and ye gave Me drink; I was a stranger, and ye took Me in; naked, and ye clothed me: I was sick, and ye visited me; I was in prison, and ye came unto Me. Verily, verily, I say unto you, in as much as ye have done it unto one of the least of these My brethren, ye have done it unto Me." How

33 See The Commission of Christ to His Apostles illustrated, by Mr. M'Lean.

important then is this evidence of the preciousness of Christ to our souls! How careful should we be to cultivate brotherly love both in ourselves and others! "Above all things put on charity, which is the bond of perfectness;" the sweetest, the most effectual, the most perfect, and the most lasting bond, that ever united the hearts of men together.

SECTION 13

HIS INTEREST IS PRECIOUS.

It is not enough for a man to talk in high strains of the melting and moving of his affections to the Redeemer, to tell of the inward experiences he has had, at certain periods, of love to Him, how his heart was drawn out to Him at this or the other time, when, in the general course of his life, he is indifferent to the cause of Christ, and unwilling to lay out Himself for the promoting of His kingdom among men. We are to make it manifest that Christ is precious to us, by constant endeavours to advance His cause and interest in the world.

Transient elevations of mind may easily produce words of affection and kindness; but words are cheap, and religion is more easily expressed in lofty professions than in actions. A practical, steady, and persevering regard for Jesus Christ, is a costly and laborious thing. It requires much self-denial and vigorous exertions in our daily walk. Men are much more easily brought to talk about the Saviour of sinners, than to live to Him.

We find the true spirit of Christianity, as has been observed on the other occasion, fully exemplified in the apostle Paul. He did not satisfy himself with those strong and ardent expressions of love to Christ, with which his epistles every where about; he exerted himself to the utmost of his power in promoting the interest of the Redeemer.

He expected nothing in so doing but poverty, contempt and hardship. He was so poor, that he was frequently under the necessity of working with his own hands for a morsel of bread. He cheerfully submitted to hunger and nakedness, stripes and imprisonment; he was content to be counted the filth of the world, and the off-scouring of all things, amidst his unwearied attempts to glorify his divine Master, in the conversion of sinners, and the edification of those who had believed through grace. He had established the kingdom of Christ in Asia; he had reduced many of the inhabitants of Macedonia and Achaia to subjection to the gospel: he had erected the standard of divine truth in Arabia; yet he purposed in the Spirit to go to Spain, and then to Jerusalem, saying, "After I have been there, I must also see Rome." The universe at large is but just sufficient to be the field of his vigorous exertions in the good cause. He included in the plan of his apostolic labours, the metropolis and the boundaries of the known world.[34]

In this way did this exalted and heavenly man make it manifest that Christ was precious to him. And are there left to us no opportunities of proving the sincerity of our attachment to Him? The same spirit which actuated this noble champion, should actuate us, according to our capacity and ability, in the more contracted sphere in which God's providence hath fixed us.

A period will certainly commence, when the kingdom of Christ shall prevail far and wide; the earth shall be full of the knowledge of the Lord, as the waters cover the seas. All the ends of the earth shall see His salvation. Princes shall be subject to the Redeemer's sceptre, and Ethiopia shall stretch forth her hands unto God. The fulness of the Gentiles shall come in, and all Israel be saved. Our Lord has taught us to pray that His kingdom may come; and those who make mention of the Lord should not keep silence; they should continue to present their ardent petitions to

---

34 Hervey.

Him, and give Him no rest, till He establish His church through the nations, and make her a praise in the earth.

If four hundred millions of our fellow-men are yet involved in heathenish darkness worshipping the host of heaven, or bowing to stocks and stones, the works of their own hands, the love of Christ should constrains us to exert ourselves in the promotion of such means as are most likely to bring them to the knowledge of the true God, and of His Son Jesus Christ. We should not satisfy ourselves barely with praying for this event. The appointed methods are to be tried, for the accomplishment of it, in a dependence on God, and under the guidance of His merciful providence. The gospel is ordained to be preached to every creature, that its sound may go out through all the earth, and its words to the ends of the world.

Many awful events have taken place in Europe, of late years, and what will be the issue of present commotions, it is impossible for such short-sighted creatures as we are to determine. Our Lord has put a check on our too curious inquiries into futurity, by saying, "It is not for you to know the times or the seasons, which the Father hath put in His own power." Two circumstances, however, may serve to encourage the hearts, and to raise the expectations of praying people: Amidst the desolations of war, and the daring efforts of infidelity and irreligion, we have seen on the one hand, a surprising blow given to the root of popish tyranny;[35] and, on the

---

35 The capture of *Rome*, the expulsion of the Pope, the overthrow of his secular dominion, and the almost total annihilation of what has been called his spiritual influence, are surprising events; and they have been effected in a manner equally strange and mysterious. That superstition which produced infidelity, and which, for many ages, had nourished it, and promoted its growth in the minds of multitudes, is, in these eventful days, falling by the hands of its own offspring, and its expiring groans resound in every direction. God hath His way in the whirlwind, and in the storm. The wrath of man shall praise Him, and the remainder of wrath will He restrain. *Babylon* is fallen, is fallen! And the instrument of her destruction is infidelity, the fruit of her womb. In like manner, it will hereafter be seen, in all probability, that war itself will be the means of destroying the military system, and of establishing the universal reign of righteousness and peace; when swords shall be beaten into plough-shares, spears into pruning-hooks, and the nations learn war

other, the zeal of professing Christians, of various denominations, revived, respecting the advancement of Christ's kingdom, both at home and abroad. It is pleasing to hear of the efforts made in different parts of this nation, to turn men from darkness to light, and from the power of Satan unto God, by publishing the gospel, and causing it to be published in towns, villages, and neighbourhoods, where it was not known. Societies are formed for the support of itinerant preachers. May the Lord of the harvest send forth labourers, and graciously succeed the pious endeavours of all those who are engaged in this good work.

Multitudes among us are likewise deeply and earnestly concerned for the heathen nations, that they might be brought to see the light of life. Liberal contributions are made in different places, for the support of missionaries. Many individuals have been made willing to leave their dearest relations, to give up all worldly prospects, to put their lives in their hands, and to encounter all the hazards and dangers to which they may be exposed, in transporting themselves to the most distant parts of the earth, in order to spread abroad the savour of the knowledge of Christ amongst the benighted nations. The expense attending these undertakings must of course be considerable; he, therefore, to whom the cause of the Redeemer is precious, has a fair opportunity of manifesting his regard for it, by contributing according to his ability, for the promotion of it.

It is well known that the efforts of men will not be successful, without the displays of Almighty Power; but this is no reason why the means which infinite wisdom hath ordained, should not be tried; and since the hearts of so many pious persons of different persuasions, and in places far distant from one another, are, at this period, affected in the same way, there is reason to hope that a

---

no more. O God! How unsearchable are Thy judgments; Thy ways are past finding out! Confusion hears thy voice, and wild uproar Stands rul'd.

Divine hand is in the work, and consequently, that the issue will, in due time, be favourable.

Reader, is the interest of Christ precious to you? Let me then ask, What have you contributed, in the way above-mentioned, towards the promoting of it? Poverty is commonly pleaded in such cases, as an excuse; but it is of no avail in the sight of God, since, if His word be true, to give is the way to get, and to scatter, the way to increase. The poor widow, who cast her two mites into the treasury, in the account of God, cast in more than all the rest. That Jesus whom we profess to love, hath said, "Give, and it shall be given unto you: good measure, pressed down, and shaken together, and running over, shall men give into your bosom. For with the same measure that ye mete withal, it shall be measured to you again."—"If there be first a willing mind, it is accepted, according to that a man hath, and not according to that he hath not."[36]

SECTION 14

HIS DAY AND HOUSE ARE PRECIOUS.

For the illustration of this let the reader attentively observe the spirit and import of the following passages: "One thing have I desired of the Lord, and that will I seek after, that I may dwell in

---

36 When the design of the mission into *India* was first made known, in the year 1793, the author of this book, in a short time, received contributions for the purpose, to the amount of two hundred pounds, which he immediately transmitted to the treasurer. Smaller sums have, since that time, annually passed through his hands, as may be seen in the Periodical Accounts, published by the society. The missionaries, three in number, are labouring with indefatigable zeal, and patient perseverance, in prayer to God, and constant preaching to the native *Hindoos*, to bring them to the knowledge of Christ. Great numbers attend their ministrations, and there is some hope of success; but as the harvest is great, and the labourers few, two other missionaries are to be sent the present year, (1799.) The New Testament, translated into the *Bengalee* language, by the unwearied application of our missionaries, is designed to be printed, and copies of it dispersed among the natives, as soon as possible. And as great additional expense will be incurred by these measures, it is humbly hoped, that those to whom the interest of Christ is precious, will manifest their concern for the promoting of it, by exerting themselves on the present occasion.

the house of the Lord all the days of my life, to behold the beauty of the Lord, and to inquire in His temple. As the hart panteth after the water-brooks, so panteth my soul after Thee, O God; my soul thirsteth for God, for the living God: when shall I come and appear before God! My soul thirsteth for Thee, my flesh longeth for Thee, in a dry and thirsty land, where no water is: to see Thy power and Thy glory, so as I have seen Thee in the sanctuary. How amiable are Thy tabernacles, O Lord of hosts! My soul longeth, yea, even fainteth for the courts of the Lord; my heart and my flesh cry out for the living God." The pious man, sensible of the diseases of his mind, waits with eagerness and constancy at the pool of divine ordinances for relief, in humble expectation that He who prevents the needy and the helpless with His mercy, will look upon him, and heal him.

The day which is to be spent in converse and communion with God, in the public and private exercises of devotion, must needs be precious to those who love Jesus. It is the Lord's day. The hours of it are all His own, to be employed in His immediate service. On this day we attend upon Him in His ordinances, we sing His praise, we hear the words of everlasting life, and we pay our vows to God in the presence of His people. Surely, a day in His courts is better than a thousand spent elsewhere, and we should rather choose to be door keepers in the house of God than to dwell in the tents of wickedness. Hear what He says to us by His holy prophet. "If thou turn away thy foot from (profaning) the sabbath, from doing thy pleasure on My holy day; and shalt call the sabbath a DELIGHT; the Holy of the Lord, honourable; and shalt honour Him, not doing thine own ways, nor finding thine own pleasure, nor speaking thine own words; then shalt thou delight thyself in the Lord; and I will cause thee to ride upon the high places of the earth (to rise above this transitory world, and live a heavenly life) and feed thee with the heritage of Jacob thy father; for the mouth of the Lord hath spoken it."

The several parts of public worship to be observed on His holy day, are suited to work upon our senses, and, by that means, to awaken pious affections within us. In singing the praises of God, solemnly calling upon His name, and hearing the blessed gospel, we find a variety of holy desires, hopes and joys excited, and our spiritual interests greatly promoted.

On this day we sometimes approach to the Lord's table, and enjoy that precious ordinance which is wisely and graciously designed to revive in our minds the remembrance of Him who gave His life a ransom for our souls. This institution is happily contrived to represent, in a lively and striking manner, the love, the sufferings, and the death of our blessed Redeemer, together with the benefits which we derive from them. When we unite in this solemnity, all the springs of pious affection should be let loose, while we contemplate the dying agonies of the Prince of Peace. We should feel the sweet meltings of godly sorrow, and the warmest exertions of gratitude, love and joy.

The Lord's day, and the worship of His house are precious, as they are emblematical of that happy state and world,

> *Where congregations ne'er break up,*
> *And sabbaths have no end.*

It is in the worship and service of God, that we are, by degrees, prepared for the enjoyments and employments of heaven. How glorious will that change be, when we are called from these earthly courts, to join the general assembly and church of the first-born! Here we are attended with much frailty, infirmity and sin; we are sometimes so oppressed with a consciousness of our own vileness, that we are ashamed to lift up our faces towards heaven. But there the pure in heart shall see God without confusion. Here we abide not in His tabernacles, but go and come, as visitants. There we hope to dwell as inhabitants for ever. And if the ordinances of God's house be the joy of our hearts in this world, if a day in His courts be preferable to a thousand spent elsewhere, what will be the worship and the enjoyments of heaven!

SECTION 15

HIS BENEFITS ARE PRECIOUS.

To be raised from a state of death in sin to a divine and spiritual life; to be brought out of darkness into marvellous light; to be delivered from guilt and condemnation; to be justified freely by the riches of grace, displayed in the redemption which is by Jesus Christ; to have welcome access to God; to be treated by Him as His adopted children: and to be made heirs according to the hope of eternal life; these are some of the benefits which we receive by Jesus Christ; benefits which result from His mediation, and hang clustering on His cross. And as they are of infinite value in themselves, they must be precious to those that believe. While the Christian contemplates these favours, he is often ready to say with the Psalmist, "What shall I render to the Lord for all His benefits towards me!"

These are benefits which will extend their duration and happy effects through eternity. In the bestowment of them, the God of all grace raises us from the dust and the dunghill, to set us among princes, even among the princes of His people. They are blessings worthy of Him that bestows them, and sufficient to exalt the riches of His abounding grace, to the admiration of all the hosts of heaven, and of redeemed men on earth. These are the things into which the angels desire to look. They will furnish matter of admiration, joy, gratitude and delight to those who are interested in them for ever and ever. How they are affected with them, and how precious they are in their estimation in this world, may be learnt from their own language: "Bless the Lord, O my soul, and forget not all His benefits. Let all that is within me bless His holy name. Who forgiveth all thy sins, and healeth all thy diseases. Who redeemeth thy life from destruction, and crowneth thee with lovingkindness and tender mercies. Blessed be the God and Father of our Lord Jesus Christ, who hath blessed us with all spiritual blessings in heavenly places (or things) in Christ; according as He hath chosen us in Him before the foundation of the world, that we should be holy and without blame before Him in love. Behold, what manner of love the Father hath bestowed on us, that we should be called the sons of God! It doth not yet appear what we shall be; but we know that, when He shall appear, we shall be like Him; for we shall see Him as He is."

In the day of His glorious appearance, He will receive us with acclamation of joy and triumph into His own palace in the new Jerusalem, where we shall have the bright vision of His face, and be made partakers of such exalted felicity as it cannot now enter into our hearts to conceive. There are no benefits like those which our divine Redeemer bestows; there are none to be compared with them. How precious are Thy thoughts and designs of love unto me, O God, how great is the sum of them!

SECTION 16

HIS CHASTISEMENTS ARE PRECIOUS.

The believer's love to Jesus Christ, not only continues under the rod of correction, but is quickened and increased by it. Thus it is distinguished from that pretended love, which subsists only in prosperity. The afflicted Christian is enabled to consider, that whom the Lord loveth He chasteneth, and scourgeth every son whom He receiveth, and that He afflicts us not for His own pleasure, but for our profit, to make us partakers of His holiness.

The Lord can so manifest Himself to His afflicted people, and cause His goodness to pass before them in such a manner, that the season of affliction shall be to them a season of great consolation. He is to them a fountain of life, of strength, of grace and comfort in the trying hour, and of His fulness they receive, as their necessities require. The men of the world are totally ignorant of these Divine supports. As they have no guide in the time of prosperity, but are carried along with the stream towards the gulf of perdition, so in adversity they have no resource, but must feel all the bitterness of affliction, without finding Divine support under it, or deriving spiritual advantage from it.

The Lord Jesus Christ is a sun to enlighten and cheer His afflicted followers, and a shield to defend them. He is a hiding-place from the storm, a covert from the temptest, and as the shadow of a great rock in a weary land.

All the afflictions of His people are designed, under His gracious management, to prove, to make manifest, and to exercise those graces and virtues which He has implanted in them. Though afflictions in themselves are not joyous but grievous, nevertheless they yield the peaceable fruits of righteousness in them who are exercised thereby. They serve to quicken the spirit of devotion in us; to rouse us from that formality and indifference which frequently attend a long course of case and prosperity. We are constrained to seek God with sincerity and fervour, when His chastening hand is upon us, since we then feel our absolute need of that help and deliverance which He only can give us.[37]

---

37   When the loss of a temporal enjoyment casts us into excessive despondency and dejection, it is evident that what we have lost was the object of our inordinate love. The most innocent attachments cease to be innocent, when they press too strongly upon us. To cleave to any created object, and to look for happiness from it, is to set it up in God's throne, and make an idol of it. Should this object be a friend, a brother, a wife, or a child, the idolatry is still odious in the eyes of that God to whom we owe our chief affection. Our warmest passions, our most fervent love, our desire, our hope, and our confidence, should always have Him for their object.

They serve most effectually to convince us of the vanity of all that this world can afford; to remind us that this is not our rest; and to stir up our desires and hopes respecting our everlasting home. They produce in us a spirit of sympathy towards our companions in tribulation. They give occasion for the exercise of patience, meekness, submission, and resignation. Were it not for the wholesome and necessary discipline of affliction, these excellent virtues would lie dormant. How then could it be known by ourselves or others, that we have the mind in us which was also in Christ Jesus? They serve to convince us more deeply of our own weakness and insufficiency, and to endear the person, the grace, the promises, and the salvation of our Redeemer, more and more to our hearts. Thus we are taught to esteem His very chastisements precious, on account of the benefit we derive from them; even as Moses esteemed the reproach of Christ greater riches than the treasures of Egypt; and the apostles rejoiced that they were counted worthy to suffer shame for the name of Jesus: "We glory in tribulation also, because tribulation worketh patience, and patience experience, and experience hope."

An eminent French Protestant writer says, "Love to God is not only continued in a Christian under the rod of correction, but it is inflamed, or increased; contrary to that false love which subsists only in prosperity, and is quite extinct in adversity. For false love in religion flows only from temporal interest, and is dependent on irregular self-love; but true love to God regards His glory and our salvation, two things which can never be separated; because

---

The perfect felicity of the saints, in the life to come, will consist in the enjoyment of God! And it is His pleasure that their present happiness should not centre in any of the good things of this life. Losses and disappointments are the trials of our faith, our patience, and our obedience. When we are in the midst of prosperity, it is difficult to know whether it is a love for the Benefactor, or only for the benefits which attaches us to religion. It is in the midst of adversity that our piety is put to the trial.

Affliction is the good man's shining scene.

God has united them so, that they constitute the very essence of religion. Whenever, then, it pleases God to chastise us, these two great interests, His glory and our salvation, present themselves before our eyes; and whether we consider chastisements as the fruits of our own sins, which have offended God; or as paternal strokes, to establish us in holiness, they cannot but serve to promote our love. Add to these, that, when a believer sees his God frown, he cannot but fear, in some sense, that His wrath will go farther. Hence these expressions of the Psalmist, 'Forsake me not, O Lord; O my God, be not far from me!' When he is apprehensive that God will forsake him, he stretches forth the arms of his love towards Him, he weeps on His bosom, he follows the example of the two disciples with respect to their Divine Master, 'they constrained Him, saying, Abide with us.' "[38]

Afflictions are not to punish, but to purify the believing soul. They are not in wrath, but in mercy. Amidst the distresses and miseries of life, it is a felicity to belong to Him, without whose permission or appointment no evil can befall us; who only permits afflictions for our good, who knows by experience what it is to suffer them, and whose kind hand will speedily put a period to all the pains we feel, when we have derived from them all the good He intends to do us by them.

An ungodly man, in affliction, is like a ship at sea in a storm, without pilot, without anchor, without cable, chart, or compass, or even the most distant view of the haven of rest and safety. It is far otherwise with the afflicted believer. The stormy winds and raging waves of the ocean, in all their fury, beat upon his little bark, and he sometimes cries, "All Thy waves and Thy billows are gone over me; my strength and my hope are perished from the Lord!" But in this distress he is still supported, when he is enabled to reflect, that his God and Father sitteth upon the floods, and

---

38 Mons. Claude.

ruleth the raging of the sea; that all the waves thereof are at his direction, and though they seem to threaten his ruin, they shall answer the purposes of his final safety, by bringing him nearer and nearer to the haven where he would be. He has much satisfaction from a review of his chart and compass; he perceives that he is in a right course, though for the present the sea be rough and stormy. His anchor too is good, his pilot is able and skilful; he confides in him who sits at the helm, with the greatest security, and at some seasons, the wished-for port of peace and rest appears in view. He then rejoices in prospect of the triumph which will attend his safe arrival, when he shall ride into the harbour, amidst the acclamations of those who are waiting to receive him, to partake of their unmingled joy, and live in eternal repose.

How many, how suitable, how sovereign are the supports our heavenly Father affords to His afflicted children! They make the affliction, which in itself would seem heavy and tedious, appear to be light, and but for a moment. It is happier to be in the furnace of affliction with these supports, than to be in the highest prosperity without them. Blessed with the hopes and comforts of religion, the true Christian would prefer the lot of Lazarus, with all the poverty and distress which he endured, to that of the rich man, who, amidst all the splendour and affluence which this world could afford, lived a life of alienation from God, and destitute of the sovereign supports which can be enjoyed by those only who love and fear Him.

SECTION 17

HIS EXAMPLE IS PRECIOUS.

Among all the advocates for morality which ancient or modern times have furnished, we cannot find one complete pattern of purity. But in Jesus we have a perfect example; an example which has the force of a law, and contains the strongest inducement to holiness. We see, in our Divine Leader, the several precepts of God's word drawn out in living characters. We behold them reduced to practice, and represented to the life, in the whole of His conduct towards God and man. We see one in our nature, amidst all the assaults of temptation, amidst all the opposition which malignity could invent, and all the allurements of this guilty world, behaving in a manner exactly agreeable to the dictates of the Divine law, and leaving us an example that we should follow His steps. And surely it must be delightful, not only to contemplate His character, but, to the utmost of our power, to imitate the most perfect pattern that ever was exhibited. It must be desirable, by constant and strenuous exertions, according to our measure, to endeavour to trace the steps of His lovely feet. "He that saith He abideth in Him, ought himself also to walk even as He walked."

It is impossible to contemplate the character of Jesus, with serious and devout attention, and not be charmed with it. We see in Him all the human passions in the highest perfection. His joys were grave, His griefs were just; His gentleness and His severity, His inflexibility and His humanity, were in perfect harmony with each other. He discovered great tenderness and genuine affection on all occasions. Sensibility to human woe was His real character.

As He did no sin, neither was guile found in His mouth, so, on the other hand, every shining virtue was exemplified in Him to a very high degree. His lowliness and meekness; His contempt of the world; His heavenly temper; His love to the Father, and zeal for His honour; His activity and diligence in doing good; His submission to the Father's will; His patience amidst the heaviest and severest sufferings: His constancy in the exercises of retired devotion; and His praying for His enemies who spilt His blood, can never be sufficiently admired.[39]

---

39 The command of Christ is our rule, His life is the copy which He hath set us. If you

Let me imitate His example and goodness, now He is seated on His throne of glory. Has He pardoned my sins? Let me learn to forgive my offending fellow-creatures. Has He had patience with me, and borne with my manners from year to year? Let me strive to exercise patience towards ungrateful men. Does He scatter His favours abroad, and communicate felicity to His creatures? Let me imitate Him in being ready to distribute. Is He continually mindful of me, are His cares for my welfare and salvation incessant? Let me be concerned for the present and everlasting well-being of others, who are united to me by the ties of nature, of society, and of religion.

Mark His unwearied activity through the whole of His life in this world. He who laid the foundations of the earth, and by His excellent wisdom made the heavens, who shakes the system He has made, and the pillars thereof tremble; who seals up the stars, and speaketh to the sun, and it shineth not: He disdained not to fix a mark of honour upon industry and diligence, being employed in the humble occupation of a carpenter, before He entered on His public ministry. The Jews said of Him, "Is not this the carpenter?"

O Christians, fix your eyes intensely on the great exemplar. Thus you will, through Divine grace, daily grow in love with

---

would walk holily, you must not only endeavour to do what Christ commands, but labour to do the work as He did it. Let the various actions of your lives be performed in a holy imitation of Him. Thus you will represent Christ on earth, and hold Him forth to all that see you.

Set Christ in His holy example before you, as the painter would the person whose picture he intends to draw. This is a pleasant and efficacious way of maintaining the power of holiness.

When you are tempted to any vanity, set the blessed Redeemer before you, consider His example, and ask yourself, "How would my Lord and Master have acted in such a case? Would He have spent His time upon such trifles? Would He have spoken so and so, or done this or the other thing which I am solicited to do? And shall I give way to that which would be a manifest deviation from His example?" God forbid.

meekness, patience, and lowliness of heart. Can you grow angry and impatient at trifles, when you view the Son of God enduring such contradiction of sinners against Himself, without the least complaint? Can you repine under any afflictions, though ever so severe, when you consider, how it pleased the Father to bruise the Son of His love, while he, with divine submission said, "O My Father, if this cup may not pass from Me, except I drink it, Thy will be done!"

The more I contemplate His amiable character, while He sojourned on earth, the more I am delighted with it. To have the same mind in me which was also in Christ Jesus, and to tread in His steps, should be my constant aim. Those who are received by Him to the possession of everlasting felicity in heaven, have humbly traced His footsteps upon earth. Of them it is said, "These are they which follow the Lamb whithersoever He goeth." They are led by Him, even in the celestial world, to the enjoyment of ever-new delights, and of pleasures for evermore.

Blessed Saviour, may Thy holy example be ever before mine eyes, in its most illustrious and transforming light! O that all the devout affections which reigned in Thy heart when Thou didst sojourn with men upon earth, might also, in some measure, reign in mine. O that I could copy out the wonders of Thy zeal for the honour of Thy Father, and of Thy love and compassion for the sinful and miserable sons of men. Thy holy affections were engaged in every act of worship, with divine ardour and fervency. I am ashamed to think of the coldness, the dulness, and the formality of my prayers and praises. O let the sacred fire of true devotion be kindled in my bosom. Melt down my hard and unfeeling heart, and mould my spirit after Thy likeness. Inflame my whole soul with love to Thee, as a happy preparative for the enjoyment of Thy presence in glory.

Chapter Five

Improvement Of The Subject

1. What has been said on this subject may serve to convince us, that the evangelical system is a righteous and an equitable one. It has been objected against it, that while faith in Jesus Christ is so much insisted on as a point of distinction between the good and the bad; the grand criterion, by which the states of men will be finally determined, we derogate from the holiness and justice of God as if He paid no regard to their dispositions of mind, or their moral characters. It appears, from what has been advanced, that none possess any moral excellence in themselves previously to their believing in Jesus Christ, with the faith of the operation of God; but that divine grace produces a difference; and such a difference, as proves that the *Judge of all* acts agreeably to His own perfections, both when He saves, and when He condemns.

It will be found at last, that the real cause of men's rejection of the truth, is, a rooted aversion to that purity of heart and conduct which it requires. "This is the condemnation, that light is come into the world, and men loved darkness rather than light, because their deeds were evil. For every one that doeth evil hateth the light, lest his deeds should be reproved." This is a plain account why so many continue in unbelief; an account which cannot be controverted. Sinners are obstinately attached to wicked habits; they stumble at the word, being disobedient; this is the grand reason assigned for their infidelity. On this ground, if they are not happily brought to repentance, the sentence of condemnation will be pronounced against them at last; and the equity of it will be acknowledged by angels, and the whole assembled world.

On the other hand, while the true Christian is justified freely by Divine grace, he is, at the same time, renewed in the spirit of his mind. In consequence of this, a total change of conduct takes place; old things pass away, behold, all things become new. To him that believes, Jesus is precious; this is evidently proved by the whole of his behaviour, both towards God and man. And at the last day, though he will be far from preferring any claim of merit, yet his works will be taken notice of, as the fruits of his faith, and as evidences of the sincerity of his love. His holy practice will then be a public and undeniable testimony, that God hath saved him in a way perfectly consistent with that love of righteousness which is essential to His nature.

> *Their faith and works brought forth to light,*
> *Shall make the world confess*
> *My sentence of reward is right,*
> *And heaven adore my grace.*

2. We hence see how necessary it is, that men should be thoroughly convinced of their absolute need of such a Saviour as Jesus is. He is precious to none but those who know that they are absolutely undone without Him. To you that believe, He is precious; but no man believes in Him without a sense of need. Sufficient proof of this has already been offered.

Sinner, you have violated the holy, just, and righteous law of God, your Maker and Sovereign. That law condemns you for ten thousand transgressions committed against it. Look into the records of your own conscience. Consider what you have done from your infancy to the present moment. Remember that your sins expose you to the wrath of the Almighty, and render you deserving of everlasting punishment: for the wages of sin is death. You are every moment in danger of eternal destruction. Your condition is miserable. God is strictly just, and to impenitent sinners, a consuming fire. In yourself, you are utterly helpless. Nothing you can do will be of any avail for your relief. Be deeply sensible of your undone condition, your absolute misery: and know that there is no help, no salvation for you but in Christ. Without this conviction, you will remain in a state of indifferency towards Him. You will never fly to Him for refuge, as the only hope set before you; you will never believe in His name, nor love His person. You will never put a proper value on His atoning sacrifice, as that alone which delivers from the wrath to come, procures pardon, peace with God, and everlasting salvation. Consider these things with all seriousness, and without a moment's delay. Life and death are set before you; life, if you believe in the Saviour's name; death, if you disregard Him.

Consider the case of a malefactor, condemned to die for the violation of the laws of his country. The sentence is passed upon him, and the day approaches for the execution of it. His state is awful, his danger is great, but not to be compared with yours. O that you may be deeply and abidingly convinced of your perilous situation! On this conviction your safety depends.

3. It will appear, from what has been advanced, that the number of those, to whom Christ is precious, is but small. The grossly ignorant have no regard for Him, because they know not His worth. Those who are notoriously erroneous do not love Him; for they who do not believe and receive the truth of Christ, do not love His person. "If any man love Me, he will keep My words;" by His words we are to understand the doctrines which He taught,

as well as His precepts and commands. The openly wicked and profane can surely pretend to no regard for Christ. They are justly characterized *haters of God.* "His citizens hated Him, and said, 'We will not have this man to reign over us.' " All those who persecute the godly are confessedly excluded; for how can they love the Head who persecute the members of the body? To the covetous and worldly-minded Christ is not precious; for they love the world, and "if any man love the world, the love of the Father is not in him." They who are under the dominion of sin are not the persons in question; for the dominion of sin consists principally in the love of it, and, by consequence, in a willing subjection to it. Now, the prevailing love of sin is inconsistent with the love of Christ. All mere formal professors of religion, and all self-righteous persons stand excluded in this inquiry. They have confidence in the flesh, and therefore reject the sure foundation laid in Zion.

When all these different classes of mankind are set aside, the number left will be but small. Multitudes are either grossly ignorant, enemies to the truth, openly profane, persecutors of the godly, lovers of the world, under the dominion of sin, or such as make an empty profession of religion, and go about to establish their own righteousness. Hence, those to whom Christ is precious are but few. "Strait is the gate, and narrow is the way, which leadeth unto life; and few there be that find it. While, wide is the gate, and broad is the way, which leadeth to destruction; and many there be which go in thereat."

4. Let every man beware of concluding himself a believer in Christ, upon slight and insufficient grounds. The primitive societies of God's people, in all probability, had fewer mere nominal Christians among them than the churches of Jesus Christ generally have at the present day. There were not many, who, from their infancy, were trained up in the ways of religion and godliness. So

that the danger of deception is, in some respects greater now, than it was in the days of the apostles; since it is the common custom among us, to make a sort of external profession of Christianity.

But let us remember, that the true believer embraces the truths of God in His understanding, and acquiesces in them with His whole heart; His meditation is fixed on the attributes of God, and the loveliness, worth, and excellency of His Son Jesus Christ; he sets the Lord before him, and steadily aims at a conformity to His will, to His image, and to His example; and he experiences the powerful efficacy of the divine word, to establish him in virtue and holiness. I cannot be a true disciple of Jesus, unless He teach me by His grace, renew me by His Spirit, wash me by His blood, and form my heart to obey His commands, and imitate His meekness, humility, condescension, zeal, and love. I must submit to His authority without hesitation, and be ready to reduce to practice the knowledge I have of His truths and ways. True faith transforms the whole man. It delivers the sinner from the tyranny of His passions, and purifies both the heart and life.

5. As it is life eternal to know Jesus Christ, so it is death eternal to be ignorant of Him. The knowledge of Him is not only necessary to all the graces, to all the duties, and to all the comforts of Christianity, but it is necessary to the very existence of Christianity. They who know not Jesus Christ, know not the way of peace, and if they die in that state, their end will be miserable.

If you have not that knowledge of Jesus Christ which is attended with love to His name, you lie under a most dreadful sentence of condemnation. "If any man love not the Lord Jesus Christ, let him be anathema, maranatha;" that is, let him be accursed when the Lord shall come. Will he, at His coming, annul this awful denunciation? No; he will descend from heaven, in flaming fire, to take vengeance on them that know not God, and that obey not the gospel of our Lord Jesus Christ. Consider this, O thou who

hast no sincere regard for the precious Redeemer. Where wilt thou
hide thy guilty, thy defenceless head, when He appeareth? It will,
by and by, be said, "The great day of His wrath is come, and who
shall be able to stand?"

6. Consider, my dear fellow-sinner, that as Jesus Christ is the
Former of all things, you were made by Him, and therefore you
ought to love Him. He has endowed you with a rational and an
immortal soul, a soul capable of knowing and of loving Him;
and will you withhold that love from Him which He so justly
demands? Perhaps you are a professor of religion, yet if Christ is
not precious to you, your profession is unprofitable. In that divine
book called the Bible, you have the history of His life, His sufferings, and His death; you have a clear display of His dignity, His
glory, His power to save, and His infinite and unbounded love to
sinners. Can you read all this, and not love Him?

Can you love those inferior objects, in which you apprehend
there are some comparative degrees of excellence, and can you not
love Jesus Christ, who is altogether lovely, and the sum of all excellence and perfection? Do you respect those on whom God hath
conferred some measure of honour, authority and power; and do
you not love Jesus Christ, who is the Lord of Glory, and to whom
as Mediator, all power is given both in heaven and earth? Do you
respect a fellow-creature possessed of wisdom and learning, and do
you not love Jesus Christ, in whom are hid all the treasures of wisdom and knowledge? Do you esteem a man who is liberal, generous, or bountiful; and have you no love for Him, who giveth us all
things richly to enjoy, and who by giving His life a ransom for our
souls, is become the Author of eternal salvation, with all its glorious blessings and privileges? You profess to have a sincere value for
your friends, who have shewn you many acts of kindness; and you
will not love the Friend of sinners? Remember His words; "Greater
love hath no man than this, that a man lay down his life for His

friends." He only can rescue you from eternal destruction; He only can bestow upon you pardon, righteousness, peace and everlasting felicity; and shall such a friend have no place in your heart?

Do you love liberty? And can you be indifferent towards Him, whose office is to proclaim liberty to the captives, and the opening of the prison to them that are bound? There is no deliverance from the condemnation of the law, the hand of avenging justice, the tyranny of Satan, the dominion of sin, and the power of death and the grave, but by Him. Do you love peace and pleasure; and can you disregard the Prince of peace, who reconciles sinners to God, by the blood of His cross, and gives true peace of conscience, together with joy unspeakable and full of glory.

There is every thing in Christ to encourage poor sinners to apply to Him, to look for salvation in His name, and to inspire their hearts with love to His person. There are motives and arguments of every kind to excite you to choose Him for your Saviour, your friend, and your portion. You are guilty; but His blood cleanseth from all sin. You are miserable; but He is rich in mercy. You are helpless; but He is mighty to save. You are impoverished; but His riches are unsearchable. His treasures of grace are inexhaustible. Approach unto Him, be not afraid of a disappointment; He has assured you He will in no wise cast you out.

There is an inexhaustible fulness in Him, answerable to all your necessities, be they ever so many, or ever so great. He is the ever-flowing, the over-flowing fountain of living waters. He is able to do exceeding abundantly above all that we ask or think. It hath pleased the Father, that in Him all fulness should dwell; and from His fullness needy sinners receive, and grace for grace. His kindness and mercy are unbounded. If the kindness of men has a tendency to win your hearts, how much more should the infinite love of Jesus constrain you to love Him? He is the only-begotten Son, the most dearly-beloved of the Father. He is worthy of the

Father's love, who says of Him, "This is My beloved Son, in whom I am well pleased." Surely then, it is reasonable, it is highly proper that He should be the object of your love.

7. Let those who regard the comfort, the peace and the prosperity of their own souls, apply themselves to the study of Jesus Christ, and daily aspire after more knowledge of Him. All that is excellent, all that is desirable, all that is comfortable is concentered in Him. He is fairer than the children of men, the chiefest among ten thousands, and altogether lovely. O how unspeakably, how infinitely precious! It is eternal life to know Him. No knowledge so enlivening, so cheering, so comfortable as the knowledge of Christ. It is ever new, ever fresh in excellency, to those who aspire after it. If we desire to be conformed to His blessed image, we should labour to have our thoughts as much as possible, employed in contemplating His excellency; that we may be able to comprehend with all saints, what is the length and breadth, the depth and height of the love of Christ, which passeth knowledge. This is the way to increase in holiness and in happiness; or, to use the more emphatic language of the apostle, to "be filled with all the fulness of God." For "while we with open face behold, as in a glass, the glory of the Lord, we are changed into the same image from glory to glory, even as by the Spirit of the Lord."

It is not probable that Jesus Christ should be very precious to those who are not acquainted with the glorious perfections of His person, His transcendent worth, and surpassing excellency. Love is founded in knowledge. When we have suitable discoveries of His glory, our wills are inclined and determined to make choice of Him, as our Saviour, and our all-sufficient portion. And affection to Him is maintained and continued in its warmth and fervour, by frequent meditation on His person, His love, His infinite excellence and preciousness. If we lose sight of His ineffable glories, His perfect righteousness and saving power, our attachment to

Him, as the spring of our happiness, will be weakened, and the fervency of our regard for Him will be abated.

No motions of the soul are so sweet and delightful as those which are directed to the Fountain of happiness. The out-goings of the heart after Christ are pleasant, especially when He is pleased to manifest Himself unto us, as He does not to the world. There is a mixture of heavenly comfort in the love we feel to so worthy an object. "Whom having not seen ye love; in whom, though now ye see Him not, yet believing, ye rejoice with joy unspeakable, and full of glory."

8. If Jesus Christ be so superlatively precious in Himself, we have reason to be ashamed that we love Him no more. Alas! How languid are our affections towards Him who is altogether lovely, and how easily are our hearts captivated with vanity and trifles! This is matter of humiliation, grief, and sorrow. It is remarked in the life of John Mollius, an eminent disciple of Jesus, that he was sometimes observed to be in heaviness, and to weep bitterly; when his friends inquired into the cause of his trouble, his usual answer was, "Oh! it grieves me, that I cannot bring this heart of mine to love Jesus Christ more fervently."

Is not our love to the Redeemer very small, in comparison with that to which some of His followers have attained? Have not thousands of martyrs joyfully endured the most cruel pains and tortures for the love which they bore to Him? O what blessed lives did the primitive disciples of Christ live! What divine satisfaction, what heavenly splendour, what convincing power attended their practice, while their whole souls, with all their affections, were devoted to their Redeemer, and engaged in the affairs of His kingdom! They lived on earth as the heirs of heaven ought to do.

May we not justly be ashamed that we have this precious Saviour so little in our thoughts. Forgetful of Him, our thoughts range abroad on a thousand subjects to little profit, nay, often to our hurt. If we examine our thoughts for one day, how few of them have been employed upon Him who should be our highest love, and nearest our hearts! Is not this matter of lamentation? Is it not a sad indication of the indifferency of our minds towards Him? A warm and fervent love would bring Him often to our remembrance. We should say with the Psalmist, "In the multitude of my thoughts within me, Thy comforts delight my soul." Or, as he says in another place, "My meditation of Him shall be sweet; I will be glad in the Lord." Can they rejoice in the Lord alway, who very rarely think of Him? "Where your treasure is, there will your hearts be also." Every man thinks much on that which is highest in His esteem, and dearest to His affections. This is a fact the truth of which cannot be called in question. But if we judge of our regard for Christ by this rule, what reason have we for deep humiliation before Him! What slender proof do we give that He is precious to us! How low, how faint and feeble is our regard for Him!

Thought being the immediate attendant of love, where love is strong and fervent, it powerfully engages the heart to habitual musing on the beloved object. And therefore when the Psalmist says, "O how love I Thy law," he adds, "it is my meditation all the day."

Is it possible that we should spend any day of our lives without thinking on what Jesus Christ has done for us? His astonishing love, in becoming incarnate, sojourning more than thirty years in this wretched and miserable world, as a man of sorrows, for our sakes; His fulfilling all righteousness for us; His enduring the contradiction of sinners against Himself; and His laying down His life in our stead, are subjects of contemplation upon which our minds should perpetually revolve.

We should think on what He is now doing for us in heaven; for He is gone there to prepare a place for our accommodation, and He ever liveth to make intercession for us. He tells us He will never forget us, and shall we perpetually forget Him? Hear what He says, "Can a woman forget her sucking child, that she should not have compassion on the son of her womb? Yea, they may forget, yet will I not forget thee. Behold I have graven thee on the palms of My hands; thy walls are continually before Me."

It is a proof that our love to the Redeemer is but small, when our tongues are rarely employed in speaking of Him. We all know, that the subject which lies nearest our hearts will frequently slide upon our tongues, and employ our discourse. The man of pleasure talks much of his carnal delights; and the man of business, of the affairs of commerce. "He that is of the earth, speaketh of the earth; for out of the abundance of the heart the mouth speaketh." The man of news talks perpetually about that in which he most delights. And have we nothing to say about Him who rescues our souls from everlasting destruction, and gives us a lively hope of full felicity in heaven?

Have we not reason to be ashamed of our negligence as to the retired exercises of devotion? How little time do we spend in those exercises, and how little pleasure do we often take in them! Alas! I fear our closets bear witness against us, concerning the deficiency of our love to Jesus Christ. Did we love Him with a fervent affection, we should often retire from the world, that we might converse with Him, and pour out our hearts before Him. A slight performance of the duties of the closet, is a certain indication that our love to the Redeemer is but small. Conscience! discharge thy office; testify against the negligent reader, how greatly deficient he is in his love, in this one instance. Tell Him of the greatness of the Saviour's love, what He hath done, what He hath suffered on His account, and what poor returns of affection are made to Him. Tell the negligent professor how inattentive he is to the Redeemer's example in this particular. Tell Him what poor, what lifeless, what slight devotions he pays to that loving Saviour, who hath promised such great things to those that seek Him with their whole hearts.

Have we not reason to be ashamed, that we are so prone to faint in the day of adversity, and to shrink back when we are called upon to take up our cross in following Christ? Had we fervent love to Him, we should, with courage and fortitude, endure great afflictions and trials in our way to the everlasting enjoyment of Him. It has induced many to glory in tribulation, to rejoice that they were counted worthy to suffer shame for the name of Jesus, to take joyfully the spoiling of their goods, and to esteem the reproach of Christ greater riches than all the treasures which this world can afford. Under the influence of this, a dungeon has been accounted a paradise, a prison a palace, and death the gate of life. Some have embraced the stake to which they were bound, and welcomed the flames by which they were to be consumed to ashes. If we therefore faint in our day of adversity, which scarcely deserves to be mentioned, in comparison with what many have endured, it is an indication that our strength is small.

9. Let your knowledge, your faith, and your love influence your practice. Shew to the world around you, that Jesus is indeed precious to you, in a constant endeavour to glorify Him, by a conversation of meekness and holiness, a life unspotted and divine. Nothing convinces like facts. Let the powerful operation of the Redeemer's love upon your hearts be seen in all your intercourse with mankind; and upon every occasion, let it be made manifest, that you neither have believed nor run in vain. The pure faith of a Christian, illustrated by works of grace and righteousness, supported under innumerable difficulties and temptations, and carried on to a death of triumph and joy, is a proof of the truth and reality of the religion of Jesus, which most effectually puts to silence the ignorance of foolish men.

Christ hath in some sense, entrusted His honour to His followers. They profess to be His friends, and His advocates on earth. Hence they should be particularly cautious and watchful, lest His worthy name be blasphemed through their misconduct. You will best vindicate His honour, and set forth His preciousness by a holy, humble, and heavenly conversation. See that ye walk worthy of Him, unto all well-pleasing. Thus you will adorn the doctrine of God your Saviour in all things, and make manifest the virtues of Him who hath called you to His eternal kingdom and glory. Let those who have their eyes upon you see that Christ is precious to your soul, by your zeal for His honour, your activity in promoting His interest, your readiness to deny yourselves on all occasions for His sake, your steady adherence to Him in all conditions, and your constancy in the use of all those means wherein you may expect to enjoy communion with Him.

10. Those to whom Jesus is precious have a happy lot, whatever their circumstances may be, as to the present life. Divine Providence has put a vast variety into the conditions of men. Some are rich, some poor, while others enjoy a desirable medium between the two extremes. Some are placed in the most eminent stations; others live in obscurity, and are, comparatively, of little use to society. It is no dishonour for the followers of Christ to be poor in this world. Their Divine Master had not where to lay His head. But a sincere attachment to the Redeemer ennobles and dignifies the soul. None in this world are so great, and so honourable as those who love Him. They cleave to Him who is infinitely worthy of their warmest affection, and who can and will make them completely happy. "Delight thyself in the Lord, and He shall give thee the desire of thine heart." Others cleave to objects which are unworthy of the ardours of an immortal soul. They debase themselves, and will one day be ashamed of their pursuits. But neither the hope nor the love of true Christians shall ever

make them ashamed. Amidst poverty, amidst afflictions, troubles and outward distresses, they have a refuge at hand, sufficient to support them, to defend them, and to afford them everlasting consolation.

They now delight to contemplate the Redeemer's excellency, and they will confess hereafter, when they see Him face to face, and are partakers of His glory, that, while on earth, they knew nothing comparatively of His preciousness and worth. They will then all unite in that everlasting song, "Salvation to our God, who sitteth upon the throne, and to the Lamb for ever and ever." Amen.

Sacred Poetry

PRAYER

There is an eye that never sleeps,
Beneath the wing of night;
There is an ear that never shuts,
When sink the beams of light.

There is an arm that never tires
When human strength gives way;
There is a love that never fails
When earthly loves decay.

That eye is fix'd on seraph throngs;
That ear is fill'd with angels' songs;
That arm upholds the world on high;
That love is throned beyond the sky.

But there's a power which man can wield
When mortal aid is vain;—
That eye, that arm, that love to reach,
That listening ear to gain.
That power is Prayer, which soars on high,
And feeds on bliss beyond the sky!

THE DEATH OF THE RIGHTEOUS

MONTGOMERY

This place is holy ground,
World, with thy cares away!
Silence and darkness reign around,
But lo! the break of day:
What bright and sudden dawn appears
To shine upon this scene of tears?

'Tis not the morning light
That wakes the lark to sing,
'Tis not a meteor of the night,
Nor track of angel's wing;
It is an uncreated beam,
Like that which shone on Jacob's dream.

Eternity and Time
Met for a moment here,
From earth to heaven, a scale sublime
Rested on either sphere,
Whose steps a saintly figure trod,
By Death's cold hand led home to God.

He landed in our view;
'Midst flaming hosts above,
Whose ranks stood silent while He drew
Nigh to the throne of love,
And meekly took the lowest seat,
Yet nearest his Redeemer's feet.

Thrill'd with ecstatic awe,
Entranced our spirits fell,
And saw—yet wist not what we saw,
And heard—no tongue can tell
What sound the ear of rapture caught,
What glory fill'd the eye of thought.

Thus, far above the pole,
On wings of mounting fire,
Faith may pursue the enfranchised soul,
But soon her pinions tire;
It is not given to mortal man
Eternal mysteries to scan.

Behold the bed of death;
This pale and lovely clay—
Heard ye the sob of parting breath?
Marked ye the eye's last ray?
No—life so sweetly ceased to be,
It lapsed in immortality.
Bury the dead—and weep
In stillness o'er the loss;

Bury the dead—in Christ they sleep,
Who bore on earth His cross;
And from the grave their dust shall rise
In His own image to the skies.